MW01698184

Oral-Motor Techniques in Articulation and Phonological Therapy

Millennium Edition
Revised 2001

Pam Marshalla, M.A., C.C.C.
Speech-Language Pathologist

MSL
Marshalla Speech and Language

Oral-Motor Techniques in Articulation and Phonological Therapy

Printed in United States

Marshalla Speech and Language
11417 - 124th Avenue Northeast
Kirkland, WA 98033
www.pammarshalla.com

ISBN: 0-9707060-3-0

Dedication

This book is dedicated to Dr. Suzanne Evans Morris for her pioneering research on feeding development, disorders and treatment, and her immeasurable influence on me as a therapist, lecturer and writer. Dr. Morris' insights into feeding and oral-motor therapy have been and continue to be the cornerstone upon which the entire field of oral-motor therapy for children has been constructed.

Dr. Morris, I hope you find this book acceptable and worthy.

Introduction

I have been encouraged for many years to write this book, and I am happy to be able to do it finally. This book is about oral-motor therapy, as it has been and continues to be practiced by thousands of speech-language pathologists, occupational therapists and physical therapists worldwide. I am glad to have been part of a movement which began humbly enough as an outgrowth of the need to do something more than traditional articulation and phonologically-based therapy. Oral-motor therapy has grown to be the "hot topic" of the 1990's, and it looks to be a strong component of treatment well into the next millennium.

I have taught the information contained in this volume to tens of thousands of speech and language pathologists from 1982 until the present. Time and again I have noted that many therapists cannot "see" an oral-motor problem at first. Over time, with training and experience, the eyes are trained to see that which has been occurring in children with articulation disorder all along.

As an early writer in our field once noted, "Speech is movement made audible." This is so true: speech is movement of four primary subsystems, namely, the respiratory, phonatory, resonatory and articulatory mechanisms. Articulation is accomplished through movements of the jaw, the lips and the tongue. A thorough understanding of these oral movements, therefore, is integral to our understanding of articulation and phonological development, delay, disorder, diagnosis and treatment.

Learning how to assess and treat oral movement problems is a process of studying, watching, listening and doing as skill comes with practice over time. Readers who are first learning oral-motor therapy are encouraged to work with other therapists who already have some amount of expertise in this field and to watch videotapes of treatment. Therapists will begin to understand jaw, lip and tongue control by watching many clients over several years. At some point most therapists are able to say with certainty, "This is an oral-motor problem," and "These techniques are working to facilitate improved oral-motor and articulation development."

Please Note: In the spirit of simplicity, male pronouns (he, him, his) will be used throughout the text to refer to the client.

Table of Contents

Chapter 1. Introduction to Oral-Motor Therapy	9
Speech is Movement	10
Definition of Oral-Motor Therapy	10
Purpose of Oral-Motor Therapy	10
Primary Goal of Oral-Motor Therapy	11
Therapies which Incorporate Oral-Motor Techniques	11
Goals of the Six Treatment Areas	12
General Goals of the Oral-Motor Program	13
Oral-Motor Therapy for Speech is Not Feeding Therapy	13
Relationship Between Speech and Swallowing	14
Diagnosing Oral-Motor Problems	15
General Versus Specific Oral-Motor Therapy	15
The Inclusion Rule of Oral-Motor Therapy	16
Exercises, Cues and Stimulation Techniques	16
Power of Stimuli	18
Hand-on Versus Hands-off Treatment	19
Following Sanitary Procedures	19
Length and Duration of Treatment	20
Oral Rest Position	21
Chapter 2. Principles of Movement Applied to the Oral Mechanism	23
General Concepts	23
The Organization of Motor Control	24
Sensory Components	32
Patterns of Movement Breakdown	35
Chapter 3. The Tactile and Proprioceptive Systems	39
The Tactile System	40
The Skin	40
Oral-Tactile Sensitivity Problems	41
Examining Oral-Tactile Sensitivity	43
Goals of Oral-Tactile Therapy	48
General Guidelines for Normalizing Oral-Tactile Sensitivity	49
Stimulus Guidelines for Normalizing Oral-Tactile Sensitivity	50
Organizational Guidelines for Normalizing Oral-Tactile Sensitivity	51
The Proprioceptive System	52

Proprioceptive Stimulation Techniques 52
Oral-Exploratory Play for Hands-Off Oral-Motor Learning 53
S.A.T.P.I.O.M.s 54
Sample Procedures to Improve Oral-Tactile Sensitivity 55

Chapter 4. The Jaw 59

Jaw Movements 60
Jaw Movements in Mature Speech 60
Jaw Movements in Development 61
The Jaw-Tongue-Palate Triangle 62
Diagnosing Jaw Movements 63
Deviations in Jaw Movements 63
Jaw Facilitation Techniques 64

Chapter 5. The Lips 69

Basic Muscle Review 69
Lip Movements in Speech 70
Lip Movements in Speech Development 70
Diagnosing Lip Movements 71
Problems in Lip Movements 71
Lip Retraction 72
A Hierarchy of Lip Therapy 74
Techniques to Reduce Lip Retraction 74
Tactile and Proprioceptive Stimulation Techniques to Activate the Lips 77
Feeding Therapy Techniques to Activate the Lips 78
Voluntary Lip Exercises 78

Chapter 6. The Tongue 81

Historic Divisions of the Tongue 81
Palatography 82
Differential Tongue Movements in Speech 84
Functional Zones of the Tongue 87
Stability and Mobility in Tongue Movements 87
Summary of Tongue Movements in Speech 89
A New Concept of Tongue Movement 90
Tongue Movements in Swallowing 91
The "Normal" Tongue Configuration 93
Tongue Movement Problems 94
Facilitating Basic Tongue Movement 97

Chapter 7. Putting It All Together 105

Hierarchy of the Oral-Motor Approach 105
Developmental Apraxia 108
Severe Unintelligibility 109
The Frontal Lisp 110
The Lateral Lisp 112
Facilitating Back Phonemes /k/ and /g/ 116
Facilitating Phoneme /l/ 118
Facilitating Phoneme /r/ 118

Annotated Bibliography Page125

Chapter 1

Introduction to Oral-Motor Therapy

Chapter Contents

1. Speech is Movement
2. Definition of Oral-Motor Therapy
3. Purpose of Oral-Motor Therapy
4. Primary Goal of Oral-Motor Therapy
5. Therapies which Incorporate Oral-Motor Techniques
6. Goals of Six Therapy Areas
7. General Goals of the Oral-Motor Program
8. Oral-Motor Therapy for Speech Is Not Feeding Therapy
9. Relationship Between Speech and Swallowing
10. Diagnosing Oral-Motor Problems
11. General Versus Specific Oral-Motor Therapy
12. The Inclusion Rule of Oral-Motor Therapy
13. Exercises, Cues and Stimulation Techniques
14. Power of Stimuli
15. Hand-on Versus Hands-off Treatment
16. Following Sanitary Procedures
17. Length and Duration of Treatment
18. Oral Rest Position

Oral-motor therapy became the "hot topic" in speech and language therapy in the 1990's despite the fact that there had been no formal research initiated, no textbooks written, and no courses taught at the university and college level. Oral-motor therapy had evolved through grass roots efforts on the part of many practicing speech-language pathologists who designed the ideas and began to teach them through continuing education programs.

This book presents basic information about oral-motor therapy as it is being practiced today. It includes information on the jaw, lips, tongue and the oral-tactile system. Aspects of "normal" mature oral-motor control are discussed as are ideas about development, disorder, assessment and treatment.

We begin our discussion in this first chapter with concepts about movement and its relationship to speech. In it we discuss what oral-motor therapy is, who uses it and how it is used, and we explore basic issues of diagnosis, goal-setting and treatment.

Speech is Movement

The most foundational concept of this text is that speech is movement made audible. Speech is movement of the respiratory system, the phonatory system, the resonatory system and the articulatory (meaning jaw, lips and tongue) system. Speech and language pathologists typically study the anatomy of these four subsystems of speech by learning their component parts — bones, muscles, nerves, skin — without studying movement itself. Yet it is the movements of these subsystems which allow speech to arise.

In this book we shall explore aspects of movement as they apply to the oral movements necessary for articulation and phonological skill. We shall discuss: (1) how movement is organized, (2) how movement develops over time, (3) how movement breaks down when there is disorder or delay, (4) how one inhibits abnormal movements, and (5) how one facilitates improved movements.

Definition of Oral-Motor Therapy

Oral-motor therapy, as it is practiced today, can be defined as the process of facilitating improved oral (jaw, lip, tongue) movements.

Purpose of Oral-Motor Therapy

The purpose of oral-motor therapy is to establish satisfactory and satisfying oral experiences. The term *satisfying* refers to the client. In the ideal situation, oral-motor training is done in a loving and caring environment in which clients gradually are introduced to the materials and techniques. Oral-motor training should be pleasurable and engaging for the client. It generally does no good to "force" oral-motor techniques on a client. He may come to hate them, may come to reject the therapist and may develop extreme tactile defensive behavior.

The term *satisfactory* refers to the therapist's need to be satisfied that the program and its techniques are moving a client toward more "normal" oral movement control. In therapy, fun and games themselves do not meet this specification, and neither do "oral exercises" which have no purpose. Activities in which it is clear that a client is gaining oral awareness and appropriate oral-motor control, however, do meet the criteria to make therapy satisfactory.

Primary Goal of Oral-Motor Therapy

The primary goal of oral-motor therapy is to facilitate improved oral (jaw, lip, tongue) movements.

Therapies That Incorporate Oral-Motor Techniques

There are six treatment areas today in which oral-motor techniques are utilized: (1) articulation and phonological therapy, (2) dysphagia therapy, (3) developmental feeding therapy, (4) orofacial myofunctional therapy, (5) neurodevelopmental treatment and (6) sensorimotor integrative therapy. There also has been some evidence that oral-motor techniques are being used in massage therapy and in therapies involving craniofacial manipulation.

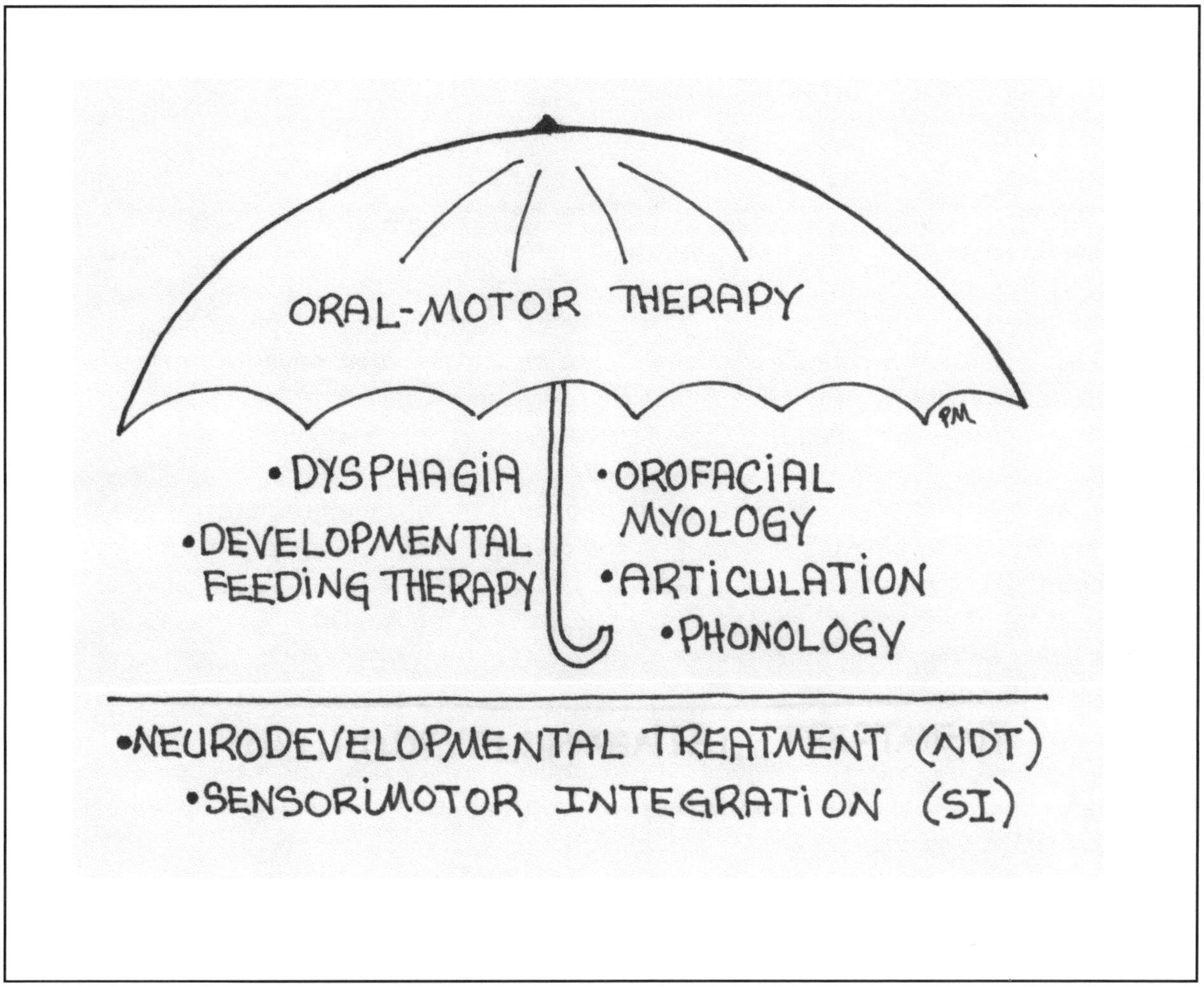

Goals of Six Treatment Areas

As stated above, oral-motor goals and techniques are interwoven throughout at least six different treatment regimes today. The goals of treatment for these areas are different but overlapping, and each includes oral-motor therapy in its daily practice.

1. Dysphagia Therapy: The goal of dysphagia therapy is to facilitate improved oral function for eating and swallowing when that function has been lost due to injury, neurological insult or disease processes. Oral-motor techniques are used to help achieve this goal.

2. Developmental Feeding Therapy: The goal of developmental feeding therapy is to facilitate improved oral function for eating, swallowing and oral exploration (including prespeech vocal play) when the normal developmental process has been or is being interfered with by congenital factors. Oral-motor techniques are used to help achieve this goal.

3. Orofacial Myofunctional Therapy: The goals of orofacial myofunctional therapy are to facilitate improved oral function in order to: (a) eliminate tongue thrust, (b) prevent functional increase in open bite or overjet, (c) improve patient's facial cosmetics, (d) sometimes move teeth slightly toward normal occlusion, and (e) help assure stability of correct occlusion. Oral facial myologists also provide therapy programs to eliminate oral sucking and licking habits. Oral-motor techniques are used to help achieve these goals.

4. Articulation and Phonological Therapy: The goals of articulation and phonological therapy are to facilitate improved oral function for better speech sound production and speech sound sequencing. Oral-motor techniques are used to help achieve these goals.

5. Neurodevelopmental Treatment (NDT): The goals of neurodevelopmental treatment are to inhibit abnormal reflex activity and to facilitate normal movement patterns in the whole body of which the oral mechanism is one part. Oral-motor techniques are used to help achieve these goals.

6. Sensorimotor Integration Therapy (SI): The goals of sensorimotor integrative therapy are to facilitate better organization and processing of sensory information from the different sensory channels, and to facilitate better ability to relate input from one channel to that of another in order to emit an adaptive response. Oral-motor skills are adaptive when we use them for eating or speaking. Oral-motor techniques are used to help achieve these goals.

Additional Areas: There are a few additional therapies in which oral-motor techniques have been included to a lesser extent. These include craniosacral manipulation, general massage therapy and acupressure.

General Goals of the Oral-Motor Program in Articulation and Phonological Therapy

The following general goals are ones which support the primary goal of facilitating improved oral movements in articulation and phonological therapy. They can be applied broadly to most clients.

1. To increase awareness of the oral mechanism and its parts.

2. To normalize oral-tactile sensitivity.

3. To inhibit “abnormal” and to facilitate “normal” oral movement patterns.

4. To increase differentiation of oral movements.

5. To achieve successful speech sound production.

Oral-Motor Therapy for Speech Is Not Feeding Therapy

As stated above, oral-motor therapy is a process of facilitating improved oral function. The techniques involved in the process can and are used in a variety of treatment regimes including feeding therapy. Oral-motor therapy as it is described in this book, however, is not feeding or swallowing therapy, and it is not intended to diagnose or treat significant feeding or swallowing problems. Readers are warned not to think of or use this book as their source of information about feeding or swallowing disorders and treatment.

Clients with feeding and swallowing disorders have health-related issues around feeding. They are *feeding-impaired* and their life and health are at risk. Feeding therapy for these clients goes well beyond simple techniques to facilitate improved jaw, lip and tongue movements. It also includes procedures regarding: (1) food and liquid preparation, (2) the use of modified bottles, cups, spoons, etc., (3) working through food texture, taste and smell groups, (4) techniques to normalize oral-tactile sensitivity and (5) procedures to facilitate better family function at mealtimes.

Children with mild-to-severe articulation and phonological deficits typically do not have feeding disorders which put their health or life at risk, and, in the traditional articulation and phonological literature, these children have not been identified as having feeding problems at all.

To the modern therapist skilled in feeding therapy, however, it is obvious that many of these children do have mild-to-moderate feeding problems. However, these children eat enough, their families are not concerned with feeding, and their health is not at risk.

I affectionately call children with subtle feeding problems *snack impaired*. These children can benefit from feeding activities and techniques which will improve their overall eating skill, but the sole purpose for including oral-motor techniques in their treatment is to facilitate improved speech. Programs and goals are designed and written to address their speech skills.

Relationship Between Speech and Swallowing

When oral-motor therapy was in its infancy, there raged a controversy around the following question: Do swallowing problems cause speech problems or vice versa? At the time, we were seeking a causative relationship between speech and swallowing to determine if therapy toward one would effect changes in the other. Perhaps, the thinking went, if we did the right type of swallowing therapy, we would eliminate the need for speech therapy.

The question itself revealed inadequate information about the nature of the relationship between the oral movements needed for speech and those needed for eating and swallowing. This relationship is not causative — feeding or swallowing problems do not CAUSE speech problems or vise versa — but the movements for each are interrelated.

We can understand this relationship between speech and swallowing when we understand how all movements are related. To illustrate this relationship, let's consider movements of the hands.

The hands (with the fingers) are able to perform many movements for use in a variety of functions. For example, our hands can hold objects, fasten buttons, cut with scissors, draw with writing utensils, poke into holes or soft substances, pull on objects, as well as signal and sign.

These sample hand movements are related to one another in that each requires a certain amount of hand and finger control. The movements themselves, however, do not cause problems for one another.

For example, problems in buttoning do not CAUSE problems in scissoring. Even on the surface this idea seems ridiculous. A child's inability to button does not CAUSE his inability to scissor; instead, poor hand and finger control cause him to have difficulty with both buttoning and scissoring. Poor buttoning and scissoring are related because each are the RESULT of poor hand and finger control. It is the poor hand and finger control which causes difficulty in both buttoning and scissoring.

Likewise, swallowing problems DO NOT CAUSE speech problems or vice versa. Both speech movements and swallowing movements are functional ways we use the mouth's movement abilities. Speaking and swallowing are related to the mouth just as buttoning and scissoring are related to the hands. Poor speaking and swallowing can be the RESULT of poor control of oral movements.

Poor oral control can cause problems in at least four functional areas: (1) speaking (articulation), (2) eating and swallowing (feeding), (3) imitating oral movements and postures, and (4) resting the oral mechanism (oral rest position). Oral-motor therapy provides therapy methods and techniques designed to facilitate improved oral movement for any of these four problem areas.

Diagnosing Oral-Motor Problems

Although this is a text on treatment and no formal evaluation tool is included, a few introductory comments about assessment should be made. The oral-motor exam goes far beyond the standard oral (oral-peripheral) exam in which structure is examined. It also goes beyond a simple checklist of the client's ability to perform selected oral movements or postures.

The oral-motor exam is an examination of habitual oral movement patterns which occur during: (1) speaking, (2) eating, (3) while imitating oral postures and movements, and (4) while engaged in other activities in which the mouth should be held at rest. These four habitual oral movement activities are the foundation of the exam.

The assessment of oral-motor abilities is almost exclusively visual. Since speech-language pathologists have been primarily trained to assess their clients' speech abilities through the auditory channel, it can take many months or years to learn to assess an oral-motor deficit completely and efficiently. By studying "normal" oral-motor control and the problems which occur in oral-motor deficits, one gradually comes to an understanding of what "normal" oral-motor control should look like.

Throughout the text information about "normal" jaw, lip and tongue control is presented. Readers can use this information to begin the evaluation process.

General Versus Specific Oral-Motor Therapy

Oral-motor therapy is like any other therapy: it is a process of treatment designed to help facilitate changes over time. Some oral-motor therapy is designed to facilitate improved overall functioning and maturity of the oral-motor system. This is referred to as *general oral-motor therapy*. General oral-motor therapy is incorporated into a client's overall speech and language program. It is a process of change which takes place over a long period of time consisting of several months or years.

General oral-motor therapy might be used, for example, in an articulation/phonology/feeding program for a young child with Down's Syndrome. This oral-motor program might include the following goals: (1) to increase awareness, differentiation and control of oral movements, (2) to normalize oral-tactile sensitivity, (3) to increase overall oral tone, (4) to increase jaw mobility, (5) to establish jaw stability, (6) to facilitate development of tongue-tip elevation and (7) to facilitate development of tongue back elevation. These goals, embedded within the client's articulation and phonological program, might blanket a treatment program of one, two or even more years.

Specific oral-motor therapy, on the other hand, is designed to use a specific type of stimulation in order to facilitate the emergence of a specific oral-motor movement for the production of a specific phoneme. Specific oral-motor therapy also is incorporated into a client's overall speech and language program.

Specific oral-motor therapy might be used, for example, in an articulation program for a child with a persistent distorted /l/. This oral-motor program might include the following goals to stimulate /l/: (1) to stabilize the jaw in a partially-open position for production of /l/, (2) to increase tone in the tongue for production of /l/, (3) to facilitate consistent tongue-tip elevation for production of /l/, and (4) to normalize oral-tactile sensitivity. These goals might be used during a few days, weeks or months of treatment.

The Inclusion Rule of Oral-Motor Therapy

Oral-motor therapy is incorporated INTO a program of articulation and phonological therapy. An oral-motor therapy program is not initiated as a means to itself; therefore, one does not eliminate other aspects of a client's articulation or phonological program in favor of doing oral-motor therapy alone. One utilizes oral-motor techniques as one engages in a program of articulation and phonological treatment.

Exercises, Cues and Stimulation Techniques

Techniques to facilitate improved oral function come in three types: exercises, cues and stimulation techniques. Various programs of oral-motor training usually are based on one or more of these types.

1. Exercises: Exercise is bodily exertion for the sake of training. When we use oral-motor exercises in therapy, we exercise movement, and an oral movement can be exercised after it has been learned. Exercises are excellent components of oral-motor training because they help clients become more familiar with movements they already can perform. There are four types of exercises which are common in oral-motor therapy.

A. Repeating Movements: Some oral-motor exercises are designed to have the client perform a movement and then repeat it multiple times. For example, when we ask a client to lift the tongue-tip to the alveolar ridge ten times in a row, we are asking him to repeat a movement. Repetition of movements increases awareness, voluntary control, strength, skill and fluency of movement. We ask clients to repeat desired movements, and we avoid having them repeat undesired movements.

B. Maintaining Postures: Some oral-motor exercises are designed to have the client perform an action and then hold the resultant posture for increasing lengths of time. For example, when we ask a client to lift the tongue-tip to the alveolar ridge and hold it for a count of ten, we are asking him to maintain a posture. Maintaining a posture also increases awareness, voluntary control, strength and skill of movement. We ask clients to maintain desired movements, and we avoid having them maintain undesired movements.

C. Lifting Weights: Athletes lift weights to make muscles work harder for movement. We can add weight to oral movement through resistance. Resisting movement also increases awareness, voluntary control, strength and skill of movement. We have clients resist desired movements, and we avoid having them resist undesired movements.

D. Stretching Muscles: Athletes stretch muscles to “warm up” — to increase blood flow and resultant oxygen exchange within a muscle, and to release pent-up energy. We can stretch the oral mechanism by opening the mouth wide, by sticking the tongue far out, by performing big oral movements and by massaging the face.

2. Cues: A cue is used to remind a client of movement. Cues can be paired to a newly learned movement and then used afterward to remind the client to use it. Cues are excellent components of oral-motor training because they can be used to teach new oral movements and they will help clients remember to use already-learned ones. Cues come in three basic types:

A. Hands-On Oral Cues: Hands-on oral cues are touch cues which therapists do on a client’s face. Hands-on oral cues teach clients what to move as well as the direction and extent of movement. For example, when we touch the upper and lower lip gently and ask the client to “close your lips” we are giving a cue. Cues do not stimulate new movement to arise necessarily, however they can be used to teach new movements, and they can remind clients what to do. The original Motokinesthetics method is an external oral cuing system, as is the P.R.O.M.P.T. method.

B. Modeled Oral Cues: Sometimes therapists use cues on their own faces to get clients to pay attention to how sounds are made. For example, we can point toward our rounded lips with the index finger to remind a client to round his lips. Modeled oral cues are an excellent addition to oral-motor therapy. They can be used to teach new movements and to remind clients of old ones.

C. Cues on the Rest of the Body: Sometimes we cue an oral movement by motioning somewhere else on the body. For example, we might tickle the arm to remind the client to produce prolonged stridency, or we might snap our fingers to remind a client to make a stop consonant very quickly. Body cues are excellent additions to articulation and phonological therapy since they help remind clients to perform newly learned oral movements.

3. Stimulation Techniques: Techniques which utilize tactile and proprioception stimulation to inhibit abnormal movement patterns and to facilitate more normal and more advanced movements are known as stimulation techniques. For example, when the tongue is completely immobile due to high muscle tone, stimulation can be given to reduce (inhibit) the tone and to encourage (facilitate) more appropriate and advanced tongue movements.

Stimulation techniques are the most powerful of an oral-motor program because they do more than simply exercise or remind a client of a movement they have learned. Stimulation techniques cause new movement to arise. This book is primarily concerned with stimulation techniques.

Exercises, cues and stimulation techniques can be used together to create a rich oral-motor learning environment for articulation and phonological training: (1) inhibition techniques take away the influence of unwanted movements, (2) facilitation techniques create new or more advanced movements, (3) cues are paired with stimulation to remind clients of newly created movements, (4) exercises are paired with cues so that over time the cue can be faded in deference to the exercise, and (5) once a client can repeat an oral movement on demand in exercise or drill fashion, he is ready to use it for the production of speech sounds.

Power of Stimuli

Inhibition and facilitation techniques are accomplished through the use of stimuli, or items used to stimulate, and stimuli are graded by their "power." The power of the stimuli refers to the influence an individual stimulus item will have on muscle contraction, tactile perception and oral movement.

Power is regulated by texture, temperature, taste, smell, vibratory nature, rate of presentation and pressure applied. Thus, individual objects in oral-motor therapy can be used in various ways and for various purposes depending on the amount of power given to them and the ways in which they are employed.

For example, a tongue depressor by itself is an item of little power. It is of little texture and is relatively neutral in temperature, taste and smell. A flavored tongue depressor has slightly more power because it is flavored, but an object such as a toothette dipped into cold applesauce will be even more powerful because it is textured, flavored and cold.

The amount of power employed in treatment is regulated by the response to the stimuli given by the client.

Hands-On Versus Hands-Off Treatment

Oral-motor therapy evolved first as a hands-on treatment program, meaning that the techniques primarily were done by therapists with their hands on clients' faces and in their mouths. Over the years, a process I like to call hands-off techniques has evolved. Hands-off techniques are those which do not require therapists to put their hand on or in a client's mouth. They depend instead on the use of toys and tools in treatment which the client can use himself. For example, hands-off techniques are preferable for groups and in situations where "scrubbing and gloving" (see below) are not possible. Both hands-on and hands-off techniques are presented in this text.

Following Sanitary Procedures

Because oral-motor therapy entails the use of hands-on and hands-off techniques, sanitary procedures are a basic practice in oral-motor therapy.

1. "Scrubbing and Gloving"

Therapists must adhere to the following hand sanitation procedures at all times when touching a client's oral mechanism either for diagnosis or treatment. We call this "scrubbing and gloving."

A. Wash with a sanitizing soap.
B. Dry with a paper towel and dispose of it, or
   dry with a cloth towel and place it in the laundry.
C. Slip hands into latex or vinyl gloves.
D. Rinse excess powder from gloves.
E. Work with the client.
F. De-glove and dispose of gloves (one use only).
G. Wash the hands again with a sanitizing soap.

Warning! Recent studies have demonstrated that clients and therapists alike can have or can develop strong allergic reactions to latex. Some of these reactions can be life-threatening. Questions about latex allergies should be a part of the initial assessment of a client with oral-motor deficit, and vinyl gloves should be substituted when allergies are noted or suspected. Many therapists opt for exclusive use of vinyl gloves for this reason.

2. Sanitizing Toys and Tools

The following guidelines must be followed when using objects on, in or around the mouth:

1. Wood objects must be used only once and then disposed of. (E.g., tongue depressors, craft sticks).

2. Paper and cardboard objects must be used only once and then disposed of. (E.g., paper towel tubes, lollipop sticks, toothettes).

3. Sponge objects must be used only once and then disposed of. (E.g., Toothettes, Ora-Swabs).

4. Cotton objects must be used only once and then disposed of. (E.g., glycerine swabs, cotton balls).

5. Plastic toys and tools can be used multiple times by the same client. Wash and dry after each session. (E.g., Bitesticks, whistles, horns, straws, etc.).

6. Rubber toys and tools can be used multiple times by the same client. Wash and dry after each session. (E.g., teething toys, Nuk massage brushes, etc.).

Length and Duration of Treatment

The length and duration of oral-motor treatment depends upon the nature and severity of the oral-motor dysfunction. The nature of the disability has to do with whether the oral-motor problems are the result of simple delay or more complex disorder.

1. Delay

In the case of simple delay, therapy should accelerate acquisition of oral-motor skill, and the ultimate goal in treatment can be to reach "normal" functioning. Length of treatment will vary depending upon how significant is the delay.

When delay is slight, such as in the case of mild articulation error on later-developing phonemes, significant changes in oral control can be seen right away — within a few sessions. In such cases, oral-motor skills will have been almost completely mature from the onset, and therapy will be a very small part of the client's initial articulation program. Oral-motor techniques may be used simply to train correct production of the specific error phoneme(s).

When delay is severe, however, changes will occur much more slowly. In the case of severe phonological impairment resulting in high unintelligibility, for example, changes in oral-motor control may come over the course of a year or more. Factors (such as severe oral-tactile hypersensitivity) may interfere for some time with oral-motor learning. Treatment for oral control can be expected to last through much of the long term of articulation and phonological treatment.

2. Disorder

In the case of oral-motor dysfunction due to neuromuscular disorder or congenital disability, therapy should work to inhibit abnormal oral-motor patterns and to facilitate more normal ones. Reaching complete normalcy, however, might not be possible. The course of oral-motor treatment probably will parallel the long course of articulation and phonological treatment, and the ultimate goal of treatment should be to facilitate the best oral control possible.

Because of the long-term needs of the client with severe oral-motor dysfunction, it is recommended that oral-motor therapy be cycled in and out of treatment on a periodic basis over the long haul of therapy. For example, a client with very low tone and severe cognitive delay may need oral-motor therapy throughout childhood. Oral-motor techniques can be included intensively on a periodic basis, and then eliminated for awhile before returning to them again. Other aspects of the communication program (e.g., work on the augmentative communication system) can be the focus of treatment during these down times.

Oral Rest Position

The term oral rest position is used to describe how the mouth should be positioned when it is at rest, or not engaged in oral movement activity like speaking, eating or imitating. For the purposes of this text, oral rest position is described in the following way:

1. Jaw: The jaw rests slightly downward so that the upper and lower teeth don't touch.

2. Lips: The lips rest gently together.

3. Tongue-tip: The tongue-tip rests gently against the alveolar ridge.

4. Lateral Tongue: The sides of the tongue rest gently on or near the palate.

5. Base of Tongue: The base of the tongue rests low.

Take a moment to observe your oral rest position. The oral rest position is the neutral position of the mouth. It is the position from which all oral movements arise.

Chapter One Summary

In this first chapter we have introduced concepts of oral-motor therapy and presented an introduction to its definition, purpose, goals, diagnosis and general procedures. We have discussed how oral-motor therapy has been and is being used in a variety of therapy programs including articulation and phonological therapy.

In the next chapter, we shall discuss how movement itself is organized and relates to oral-motor control.

Chapter 2

Principles of Movement Applied to the Oral Mechanism

Chapter Contents

1. General Concepts
2. The Organization of Motor Control
3. Sensory Components
4. Patterns of Movement Breakdown

To understand oral movement and oral-motor therapy, one must understand basic concepts about movement itself. The principles of movement selected for this chapter are ones which have been abstracted from a variety of motor therapy procedures. These are some of the basic principles of movement which occupational and physical therapists learn to practice their trades.

The principles have been organized into four basic areas: (1) general concepts, (2) the organization of motor control, (3) sensory components, and (4) patterns of movement breakdown. Each principle is explained, and examples of how the principle applies to whole body movements in general and to oral movements in specific are discussed. Applications to articulation and phonological therapy are made.

General Concepts

In this first section, we present general concepts about motor development.

1. Development is a continuous process from conception to maturity.

Motor skills, including oral-motor skills, develop throughout life and can be refined with practice even through adulthood. For example, physical activity or physical therapy can be beneficial to almost all clients regardless of age. The main exception to this practice is in the case of progressive disease in which case physical exercise may speed severity of dysfunction.

This principle applies to oral-motor therapy. Oral-motor techniques can be beneficial to clients of all ages except for those with progressive disease in which case maintaining highest level of function for the longest period of time is the primary goal. Oral-motor techniques which support this goal can be included in treatment for the patient with degenerative disease.

• Application to Articulation and Phonological Therapy: Oral-motor techniques can be considered for use with all clients regardless of age.

2. The sequence of motor development is the same for all children although the rate may vary from child-to-child.

In normal development, movements progress through a highly predictable sequence which is dependent upon emerging underlying skills. For example, most children sit before they stand, stand before they walk, and walk before they run. Some children acquire these skills very early, while others do so later, but, in general, most children acquire these skills in this sequential order.

Oral-motor skills also progress through a highly predictable sequence, and this is noted in both speaking and eating. For example, in learning to eat, most children suckle-swallow before they swallow, and use the tongue in an anterior-posterior pattern before they do so in a left-right pattern. In speaking, most children learn the oral movements for /b/ earlier than they learn those needed for /r/. This occurs in part because the oral movements required for a bilabial are earlier to develop than the oral movements necessary for /r/. The sequence of oral-motor development contributes to the order in which vowel and consonant phonemes are acquired.

• Application to Articulation and Phonological Therapy: Articulation and phonological therapy should progress in a sequence constructed with information about the development of oral movement control.

The Organization of Motor Control

In this second section, we present information about how movement is organized in development.

1. Movements develop cephalocaudally.

The term *cephalo* refers to the head, and the term *caudal* refers to the tail. Motor specialists describe movements of the body beginning at the top of the spine (near the head) and progressing down the spine toward the tailbone. In this fashion, head and upper back movements "come in" before lower back and hip movements.

Oral movements, being located at the uppermost part of the spine, are some of the earliest to develop in infancy. In fact, we expect full-term healthy babies to be ready to suck shortly after birth. Because oral movements are some of the first ones to be organized, oral-motor therapy often is the beginning point of an entire NDT or sensorimotor treatment program.

• Application to Articulation and Phonological Therapy: Oral-motor therapy can and should be done early in a treatment process for speech delay and disorder.

2. Gross motor control emerges earlier than fine motor control.

Gross motor movements are defined as those movements which require the use of large muscle groups. *Fine motor movements* are defined as those movements which require the use of smaller muscle groups.

In hand development, for example, children first use the whole hand in a gross grasping pattern well-named the gross grasp. From there children learn isolated finger control in grasping and develop a grasp known as the neat pincer. While the hands are immature and still used grossly, children cannot use a neat pincer grasp to pick up a small item. They will rely on their gross grasp even when attempting to pick up something very small.

Oral movements also begin in a gross fashion and develop into refined control over time. For example, a syllable such as /ba/ is produced in infancy with gross movements — the jaw moves up and down in large movement patterns and the lips move hardly at all. Over time, the jaw begins to move in smaller graded movement patterns and the lips become more active. The final result of oral-motor maturation is the production of /ba/ with limited jaw activity and relatively greater lip activity. Mature and refined oral control in speech allows the child to develop the rapid and sequential oral movements needed for rapid connected speech.

• Application to Articulation and Phonological Therapy: Articulation and phonological therapy should be constructed to allow for a child's developing oral control. As an example, immature productions of /s/ — those made with gross oral movement — should be expected and allowed, even praised, when stridency is first emerging. This is because the child with immature oral-motor development will attempt to add stridency in his speech before he is able to control it with the refined oral movements necessary to produce /s/ without distortion.

3. Mass movements differentiate one from another over time.

The process of developing independent use of gradually smaller muscle groups is known as the process of *differentiation of movement*. Other terms used to describe this process are *separation* and *dissociation* of movement. When a child develops from a gross grasp to a neat pincer, for example, he is learning to differentiate his individual finger movements from one another and from the hand.

The oral mechanism — being comprised of jaw, lips and tongue — first functions as a single unit. Over time the jaw, the lips and the tongue dissociate their movements one from another and become independent moving parts. Independent use of each part is necessary for production of mature speech.

For example, in mature speech, phoneme /l/ is made by elevating the tongue tip to the palate, while simultaneously lowering the jaw and parting the lips — one part goes up while two other parts go down. Without independent movement in each oral part, phoneme /l/ must be attempted in some other way.

Any first-year speech student knows that young children typically substitute /w/ for /l/, and this common substitution is easy to understand from a movement differentiation perspective. Young children cannot differentially elevate the tongue-tip while depressing the jaw and parting the lips all at the same time. Since the jaw, lips and tongue are poorly differentiated, children make the movements for /l/ more grossly by eliminating independent tongue-tip elevation. Over time, however, children gain this skill and /l/ emerges with an appropriate oral movement pattern.

• Application to Articulation and Phonological Therapy: Programs of articulation and phonological therapy should be designed to include activities and techniques to help foster differentiation of oral movements.

4. All movement is accomplished through an interplay of mobility and stability.

The term *mobility* refers to the moving part of a movement, while the term *stability* refers to its stationary part. These two terms are used relative to one another. The principle means that all movements consist of parts that are more moving and parts that are more stationary. Suzanne Evans Morris has noted that stability allows for advanced and accurate mobility. Stated in the reverse, accurate and advanced mobility is based upon appropriate stability.

For example, to use the hand to write with a utensil, the arm must be stabilized at the shoulder and the hand itself must be stabilized on or near the paper. Without hand, arm and shoulder stability, the hand will not be able to control the fine movements it needs to write legibly.

The term *stabile* does not mean "stationary," "stiff" or "unmoving." It refers instead to relative stability. The shoulders and arm stay relatively stabile during hand writing. This means that although the shoulders move a little bit, they are stabile relative to the movements the hand makes.

An interplay of mobility and stability also is needed for advanced oral control and speech. For example, the jaw must be relatively stabile so that the tongue can move in efficient movement patterns near and against the palate. If the jaw is unstabile — for example if it lateralizes or protrudes too much in speech — then the physical relationship between the tongue and the palate changes, and the tongue will be unable to hit its intended target. Relative stability of the jaw allows for accurate and advanced tongue movements to develop.

• Application to Articulation and Phonological Therapy: Programs of articulation and phonological therapy need to include the concept of mobility and stability. For example, little progress in the production of lingua sounds should be expected until after the jaw comes under relatively greater stability.

5. Movements develop from proximal to distal.

The terms *proximal* and *distal* are relative ones used to describe distance toward or away from the center of the body. *Proximal* means nearer to the center of the body while *distal* means further away from it. This principle means that movements which are made at points nearer the center of the body tend to be acquired earlier than those made further away.

For example, in general, shoulder movements develop before elbow movements, elbow movements develop before wrist movements, and wrist movements develop before finger movements.

In applying this concept to speech, we should consider all four subsystems of speech: respiration, phonation, resonation and articulation. Infant research reveals that vocalizations develop from proximal to distal through these four subsystems as follows:

• Proximal: Between birth and two months of age, babies produce sound. This is movement control at the lungs (respiration) and at the larynx (phonation), the most proximal speech subsystems.

• More Distal: By two-to-three months of age, babies begin to discover how to direct sound and air differentially out the mouth and out the nose. This is movement control at the velum (resonation), a control point more distal to the larynx.

• Most Distal: By four-to-six months of age, babies begin to experiment with sound by making movements with the jaw, lips and tongue. This is movement control in the mouth (articulation), the area most distal of the four subsystems.

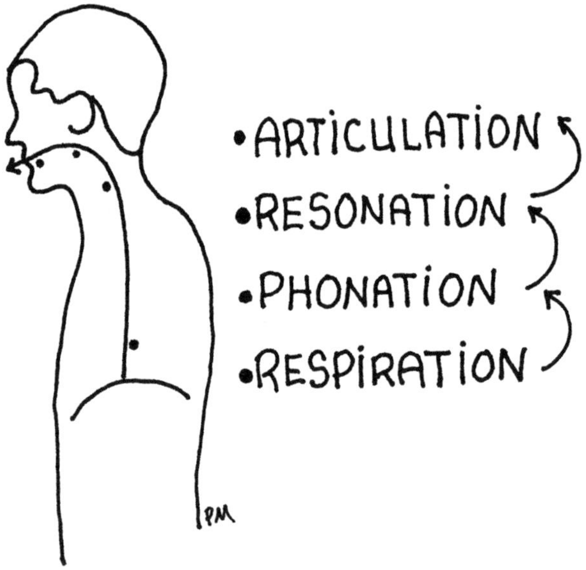

This principle of proximal-to-distal development also helps us see how children begin to learn place of articulation. For example, before true English consonants emerge, children learn to produce raspberries, and they do so at four very distinct places of articulation which are arranged from proximal to distal: (1) at the glottis, (2) at the velum, (3) with the tongue-tip, and (4) with the lips.

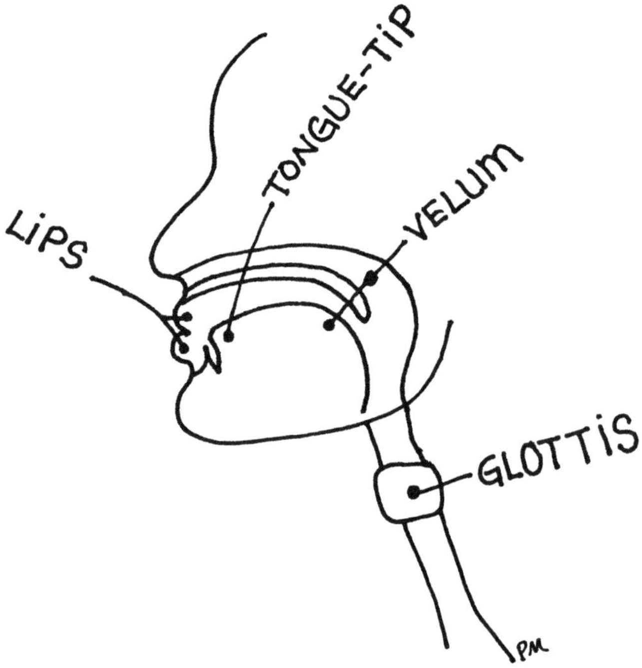

Guess which of these sounds are the earliest to emerge? You're right — those that are most proximal, meaning the raspberries produced at the glottis (we call it grunting), and those produced at the velum (we call it a velar fricative). Lingua raspberries and bi-labial raspberries come in a little later.

• Application to Articulation and Phonological Therapy: Articulation and phonological programs should incorporate the principle that oral movements develop from proximal to distal. For example, children with very little oral movement and almost no consonant phonemes might acquire back consonants /k/, /g/, /ng/, /y/ and even /r/ earlier than they are able to acquire anterior phonemes /b/, /m/ and /w/. Programs which routinely and rigidly address anterior consonants phonemes first in therapy need to be adjusted to the client who, because of oral-motor delay or deficit, is more ready to acquire back phonemes.

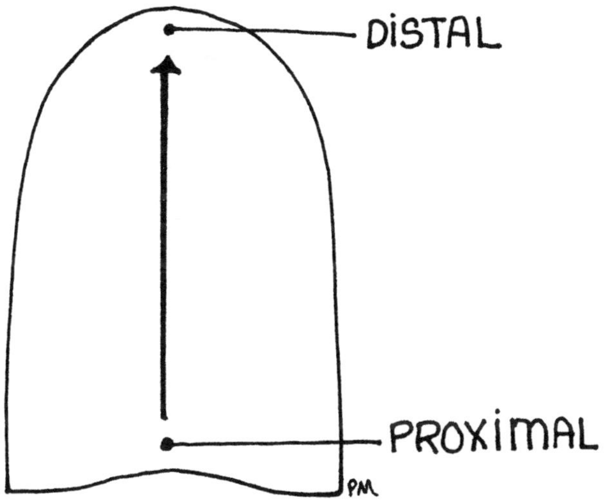

PROXIMAL-TO-DISTAL DEVELOPMENT OF THE TONGUE

6. Movement development progresses from medial plane control, to lateral plane control, and finally to rotational plane control.

The terms *medial*, *lateral* and *rotational* refer to the direction the body moves relative to a fixed position. For example, trunk control is described relative to the spine. Trunk control first is acquired in the medial plane actions of basic extension and flexion. Then, lateral trunk control develops in the form of side-to-side righting. Later, rotational trunk control emerges in which movement around the spine (turning or twisting) is acquired.

Medial, lateral and rotational plane movements also are noted in the development of oral movements, and these are seen most easily in feeding development. For example, the tongue first moves in the medial plane in an anterior-to-posterior movement pattern known as the suckle-swallow. After a few months, the tongue begins to move toward the left and toward the right along the lateral plane when reaching for food presented to one side or the other, when pushing food toward one side or the other, and finally, when transferring food side-to-side.

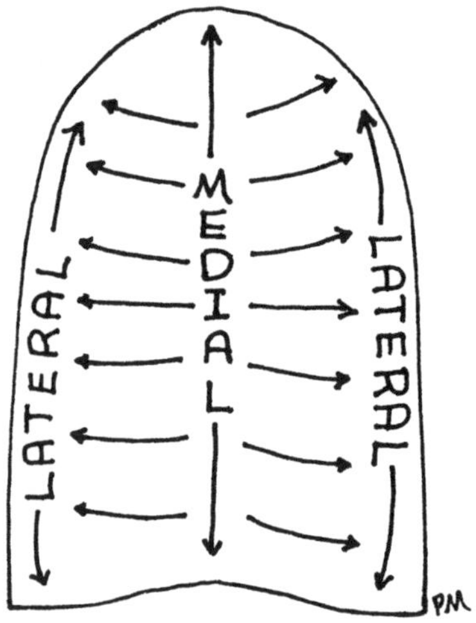

MEDIAL-TO-LATERAL TONGUE DEVELOPMENT

The ultimate way in which the tongue moves is in rotation in all directions. Rotational tongue movement is a signal that the tongue is fully differentiated from the jaw and has acquired full movement capability. With full movement capability, the tongue is ready for mature articulation skills to emerge.

- Application to Articulation and Phonological Therapy: Programs of articulation and phonological therapy need to include the concept of developing plane of movement. For example, therapy to develop tongue movements for speech needs to address movement in all planes in the order in which they emerge, even though some of the movements themselves are not used in the production of mature speech sounds.

7. Rapid and precise sequential movements are dependent upon the ability to perform discrete movements.

The concept of this principle is fairly obvious. It means that any movement which cannot be performed by itself cannot be used in a sequence of movements. For example, a child cannot throw a ball unless he can lift the arm. The child must learn to lift the arm and to perform other discrete movements before he will be able to put these movements to gether in sequence to throw a ball.

Quite obviously, the principle applies to oral-motor development. For example, when a child cannot move the lips for production of /b/, he will be unlikely to use that movement in sequence with other consonants and vowels in nonsense syllables, words, phrases, sentences or in conversation.

• Application to Articulation and Phonological Therapy: Traditional articulation therapy always has supported the concept of teaching production of discrete phonemes prior to working on syllables, words, phrases and sentences. This practice should continue in light of what we know about motor development.

8. Movement patterns are based upon economy of movement: the less effort involved, the more likely the movement pattern will be selected.

This principle means that humans tend to use those movement patterns which are easy to perform and which are economical in their use. For example, although we have the ability to spread the fingers widely apart, we almost never do so. Only when we have to — such as when we are polishing the fingernails — will we spread the fingers as widely as we are able. Humans have not developed the habit of frequently using this movement pattern during the course of everyday living events because it takes a little concentration and effort.

The same applies to oral movements. For example, although we have the ability to extend our tongues outside of the mouth to a considerable extent -- as when cleaning the upper lip -- we do not use this movement pattern in speech. It requires too much effort and is not economical. Instead, we maintain close proximity to the *neutral position* inside the mouth from which all lingual speech movements are performed.

• Application to Articulation and Phonological Therapy: Articulation and phonological therapy needs to take this principle into consideration when diagnosing and treating disorder. For example, a child with a large anterior open bite will be unlikely to articulate the upper and lower lips during production of bilabial phonemes /b/, /m/ and /p/. The client may be able to do so on isolated speech tasks, but he will be unlikely to do so in connected speech. Bi-labial articulation during the demands of rapid conversational speech will take too much effort.

Remediation for this client, therefore, must address the oral structure and oral habits which may be perpetuating the structural problem, as well as the process of learning the lip movements necessary to articulate bi-labially. If structural changes through orthodontia or oral surgery is not a possibility now or in the future, then clients often must be taught compensatory patterns, or they must be left to use their deviant pattern. When phonemes are treated without attention to what comes most easily and efficiently for a client's situation, limited success in rapid conversational speech can be expected.

9. Rhythmicity is a basic foundation and a critical component in all movement development.

In normal development, all movements develop in rhythm. As Morris and Klein have written, "We have rhythm generators in all body systems," and rhythmicity is "perhaps the most basic and encompassing issue of normal development." Rhythm allows for body systems to work in synch, and this synchronistic coordination of movements brings the efficiency needed for skill acquisition.

For example, when a child can rhythmically coordinate the movements of the head, eyes, mouth and arms, he can begin to explore objects by holding them, looking at them and mouthing them.

In oral-motor development, rhythmicity first allows a child to learn a coordinated sucking-breathing pattern and a coordinated exhalation-phonation pattern. Many months later, rhythmicity allows for the child to produce coordinated consonant and vowel sequences in babbling.

• Application to Articulation and Phonological Therapy: Programs for articulation and phonological development need to include the concept of rhythmicity as children are taught to speak and to articulate.

Sensory Components

In this third section, we describe how sensory perception interrelates with motor learning.

1. Early learning is a sensorimotor experience.

Humans are blessed with seven sensory receptors: auditory, visual, olfactory, taste, tactile, proprioceptive and vestibular. Children use their sensory perceptions about the world to help them perceive themselves and the world. In the sensorimotor stage of intelligence as described by Jean Piaget, infants learn to integrate sensations from all sensory receptors to build concepts of self, movement, objects and the environment.

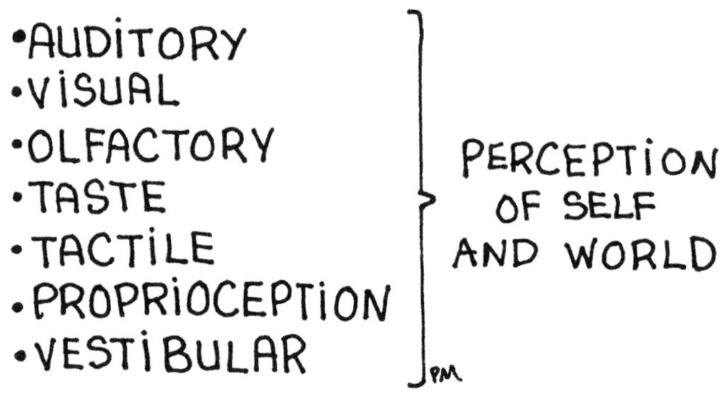

Sensorimotor learning, which predominates from birth through 18 or 24 months, is a foundational experience in early oral-motor development. Infants and toddlers engage themselves for hours upon hours of sensorimotor experimentation with the mouth in the form of mouthing, eating and vocal play.

Each object which enters the mouth in the mouthing phase is sucked, chewed, licked, smelled, and voiced on. It is banged into the mouth and gagged on, and it is pulled and pushed with the lips and tongue. This systematic mouthing play teaches infants about objects — their size, shape, temperature and texture — and it teaches them about their own mouths — its size, shape and movement capabilities.

Infants also spend an enormous amount of time "playing with" vocalizations and speech sounds during this period. This is sensorimotor experimentation with sound which functions as a foundation for the oral movement discoveries used in speech sound acquisition and phonological organization.

• Application to Articulation and Phonological Therapy: Programs of articulation and phonological therapy need to include activities to facilitate general sensorimotor and oral-motor learning experiences. In this book, this process is termed oral-exploratory play: it is described in Chapter Three.

2. Problems in the development of sensory perception can interfere with motor development.

A deficit in the function or integration of the seven sensory receptors can result in a child's inability to acquire and organize movements. For example, when a child's tactile system is impaired, especially when it reacts in a hypersensitive manner, he will limit the number and types of substances he will explore with the hands. This, in turn, affects the child's developing hand movements because his explorations with them are inhibited and limited, and his willingness to use them for a variety of activities is depressed.

Oral-motor learning also is affected by problems in sensory perception. For example, when a child is oversensitive to touch stimulation in the mouth, he gags quite easily. As a result, the child will limit the number and variety of object-to-mouth, feeding and vocal play experiences in which he is willing to engage. Without a rich oral sensorimotor, oral-motor learning experience in early childhood, the child has less general knowledge about his oral mechanism and his oral muscle tone may be low due to limited exercise. As a result, this child will be less well prepared for vowel and consonant learning.

• Application to Articulation and Phonological Therapy: Programs for articulation and phonological therapy need to include activities to enhance sensory processing so that oral-motor and phoneme learning can take place under optimum conditions.

3. Reflexes form the basis of all voluntary movements.

The term reflex refers to the relationship between stimulus input and motor output. This relationship might be expressed as a formula: Reflex = Stimulus Input + Motor Output. In other words, when sensory stimuli are given to the body, the body moves. This theory proposes that all voluntary movements have a reflex base, and that concept has been somewhat controversial in the motor therapies. For the purpose of this text, we will assume that the principle is true.

Again we turn to the hand to demonstrate this principle in action. Early hand grasping is reflex-bound: stimulation to the palm of the hand (stimulus input) causes the hand to grasp (motor output.) Over time, the reflex activity is diminished and voluntary control over the grasping pattern is acquired.

Following this principle, all oral movements have a reflex base, and this is especially easy to see when we analyze basic tongue movements. For example, elevation of the tongue's lateral margins for production of the sibilants can be traced back to the lateral tongue elevation that occurs when tactile stimulation is applied to the sides of the tongue.

- Application to Articulation and Phonological Therapy: Articulation and phonological treatment programs should include stimulation of oral reflexes when necessary to facilitate oral movement.

4. Complex motor activities are monitored through continuous sensory feedback.

The seven sensory systems not only allow for motor learning, they also allow us to monitor or keep track of our movements as they occur. For example, as we walk, our sensory mechanisms serve to tell us how we are doing. They give us feedback about the position of our legs (proprioception), the uprightness of our bodies (proprioception and vestibular), the relationship of other objects to ourselves (vision and hearing), and so forth. Continuous sensory feedback is the mechanism we use to monitor ourselves completely as we move through space.

The sensory mechanisms also allow us to monitor our speech. The proprioceptive system gives us information about our jaw, lip and tongue positions and movements. The tactile system gives us information about where and how articulation occurs in the mouth and pharyngeal area. The auditory system gives us feedback about the acoustic result of our productions.

• Application to Articulation and Phonological Therapy: Articulation and phonological treatment programs traditionally have been based on auditory training alone. Oral-motor therapy brings methods to help clients become more aware of the feedback their oral proprioceptive and tactile systems are bringing them in regard to phoneme production.

Patterns of Movement Breakdown

In this final section, we specify what happens to movement with interference.

1. When more difficult components are added to the system, the tendency is to resort to more primitive movement patterns.

When stress is added to the human motor system, movement breakdown occurs, and this breakdown is in the direction of simplicity. For example: fine motor patterns revert to gross motor ones, distal movements revert to proximal ones, and rotary movements revert to lateral ones and then to to medial ones.

Breakdown to simplicity in oral motor patterns also occurs with stress. For example, when muscle tone is high, the tongue will revert from a mature suck-swallow pattern to an immature suckle-swallow.

Breakdown to simplicity also occurs in oral-motor control for articulation. For example, when a client cannot perform the rapid sequential movements necessary for production of consonant clusters, he tends to reduce or simplify the cluster. As a result, for example, /sp/ in the word "spoon" may change to /p/.

• Application to Articulation and Phonological Therapy: The concept that speech breaks down into simpler movement patterns is a well-accepted one in speech and language therapy.

2. When development is impeded, movement can become delayed and/or disordered.

This principle means that when development is impeded by congenital factors, development of movement can be slowed down (delayed) and/or it will develop along inappropriate paths (disordered). For example, with a neuromuscular disorder like cerebral palsy, (1) movement development is slowed down, and (2) the path of development changes. Thus the child has skills which are both delayed for his age and "abnormal."

The same occurs in oral-motor development. For example, in the presence of neuromuscular disorder, children develop oral-motor skills slower and they develop "abnormal" oral motor patterns.

• Application to Articulation and Phonological Therapy: Programs of articulation and phonological therapy first need to assess if a child's speech movement patterns are developing along the right path but simply slower to evolve, or whether the child has begun to development abnormal oral movement patterns. When abnormal patterns are noted, these need to be inhibited while more normal movement patterns are facilitated.

3. Abnormal structure usually necessitates an adjustment or compensation in motor function.

Structural differences result in different motor patterns. For example, if one leg is smaller (shorter) than another, the position of the hips changes in relation to the horizontal plane which in turn causes a shift in spine, shoulder and head position. This affects all movements in the body.

In oral-motor development, any structural difference present in the mouth necessitates an adjustment or compensation in movement and posture of the jaw, lips and tongue. For example, the anterior open bite can result in an anterior tongue carriage and a frontal lisp pattern. Oral structural problems can include: fistulas, clefts, short frenums, malocclusion, diastema, missing teeth, velopharyngeal insufficiencies, surgical alterations of jaw, lips, tongue or palate, and so forth.

• Application to Articulation and Phonological Therapy: Because they will interfere with intended progress, oral structural problems cannot be ignored when designing articulation and phonological programs. In the ideal situation, all structural differences will be eliminated either before or during the course of speech therapy. When structural problems cannot be eliminated, compensatory oral movements must be taught.

4. Poor medical status can interfere with motor learning.

This principle is self-explanatory. For example, chronic heart problems can interfere with a child's ability to acquire even the most basic of movements — rolling over, sitting, walking, running and so forth. Presence of medical problems typically slows rate of development due to the medical condition itself and due to general lack of activity.

Medical problems also can interfere with oral-motor learning. For example, severe allergies and other upper respiratory problems can cause difficulty with nasal breathing which, in turn, can cause problems in jaw, lip and tongue posturing and movement.

• Application to Articulation and Phonological Therapy: In the ideal situation, all medical problems will be eliminated either before or during the course of speech therapy. When medical problems cannot be eliminated, compensation for them must be made.

5. Idiosyncratic movement patterns which are unusual, chronic, long-term and habitual can interfere with appropriate motor learning.

Repetitive movement patterns which a child acquires and "over-uses" can inhibit his ability to develop movement patterns. For example, the child who habitually flicks the hands may be slower in the development of hand movements because the hands are otherwise occupied for many hours of the day.

The same applies to oral-motor development: oral habits can interfere with oral-motor learning. For example, chronic thumbsucking can interfere with the development of appropriate tongue movements. Chronic oral habits include: excessive thumb or finger sucking, pacifier sucking, nail biting, lip licking, cheek and tongue chewing, tooth grinding, clothing or hair sucking or chewing, and so forth. Some habits will cause actual oral-structural deviation. The effect an oral habit will have on oral structure and movement depends on three factors: frequency, duration and intensity of the habit.

• Application to Articulation and Phonological Therapy: In the ideal situation, all oral habits will be eliminated before or during the course of speech therapy.

6. Abnormal tone or movement in one part of the body usually necessitates an adjustment or compensation in motor function somewhere else.

This principle means just exactly what it says. For example, low abdominal strength causes an overworking of the lower back muscles. This extra work in the back is compensation for lack of work in the abdomen.

Muscle tone problems also have a direct and powerful effect on oral movement. For example, excessive low tone in the face can cause the client to develop stiffness or tightness in some parts of the face or mouth. When the tongue is tight, for example, it is rendered less mobile, and, with less mobility, it is less able to develop the finer movements it needs to articulate a variety of phonemes correctly.

• Application to Articulation and Phonological Therapy: Treatment of oral-motor problems in articulation and phonological therapy should include techniques to inhibit abnormal tone along with techniques to facilitate improved oral control.

Chapter Two Summary

This second chapter has presented an overview of selected principles of movement development as they relate to whole body movement in general and oral movement in specific. Implications for articulation and phonological therapy have been made.

The general process of oral movement control is one of high organization in development, delay, disorder and facilitation. Thorough knowledge of principles of movement allows one to make intelligent choices about the course of oral-motor treatment and the specifics of daily practice.

Chapter 3

The Tactile and Proprioceptive Systems

Chapter Contents

1. The Tactile System
2. The Skin
3. Oral-Tactile Sensitivity Problems
4. Examining Oral-Tactile Sensitivity
5. Goals of Oral-Tactile Therapy
6. General Guidelines for Normalizing Oral-Tactile Sensitivity
7. Stimulus Guidelines for Normalizing Oral-Tactile Sensitivity
8. Organizational Guidelines for Normalizing Oral-Tactile Sensitivity
9. The Proprioception System
10. Proprioceptive Stimulation Techniques
11. Oral-Exploratory Play for Hands-Off Oral-Motor Learning
12. S.A.T.P.I.O.M.'s
13. Sample Procedures to Improve Oral-Tactile Sensitivity

Traditional articulation and phonological therapy programs have been designed around auditory and visual stimulation. Auditory stimulation is provided to increase a client's ability to hear, attend to and discriminate sound. Visual stimulation is provided to teach the client how his mouth should be positioned to say selected sounds. Many clients succeed with auditory and visual stimulation alone, but some do not.

Oral-motor therapy brings tactile and proprioceptive stimulation to traditional articulation and phonological therapy for those clients who cannot and do not progress well with auditory and visual stimulation alone. In this chapter we discuss the tactile and proprioceptive systems and their role in developing oral movement.

The Tactile System

The term *tactile* refers to sensations which arise from the skin or cutaneous tissue. As touch-sensitive beings, humans have the ability to perceive and organize touch experiences in many ways:

1. Touch Awareness: We have the ability to be aware of when we are touching and when we are being touched.

2. Touch Localization: We have the ability to identify with what part of our bodies we are touching as well as on what part of our bodies we are being touched.

3. Touch Discrimination: We have the ability to discern if an object is hot/cold, wet/dry, rough/smooth, stationary/moving, vibrating/still, or soft/hard. We have the ability to determine if we are being touched deeply, firmly or lightly, and we have the ability to determine when we are being touched in one or more places simultaneously.

4. Touch Memory: We have the ability to remember how and where we touched or have been touched.

5. Touch Sequential Memory: We have the ability to remember in what sequence we touched or were touched.

6. Touch Figure-Ground Discrimination: We have the ability to ignore a ground of tactile stimulation and pay attention to a figure of stimulation.

The tactile system informs us where our body ends, when touch experiences occur, where they occur, and in what sequence they occur. These are foundational experiences for articulation development and life-long speech monitoring.

The Skin

When speech articulation occurs, it is not bones, muscles or nerves which touch one another — it is *skin*. Skin covers the entire surface of the oral mechanism, both inside and out. When the tongue-tip touches the alveolar ridge, for example, it is not the muscles of the tongue which touch the bones of the palate. Instead, it is the skin on the upper surface of the tongue which touches the skin on the lower surface of the palate.

Skin-to-skin contact is what makes for articulation. In fact, the term "articulation" itself means to unite, to bring together, to make a joint, or to touch. The process of learning to speak is the process of learning to touch skin-to-skin in various parts of the oral-pharyngeal area while simultaneously exhaling and producing sound.

When a child develops through a "normal" oral-motor learning experience in the stage of sensorimotor intelligence, he engages in oral exploration, feeding, oral hygiene and vocal play in ways which bring him a rich experience of oral-tactile learning. This wealth of oral-tactile learning helps him to develop his ability to be aware of touch experiences as well as to localize, discriminate and remember them.

With these abilities in tact, children can learn how to produce specific speech sounds. Without that "normal" experience, children are at a disadvantage when it comes to learning speech. Many of the clients we serve in speech and language therapy have tactile sensitivity and tactile perceptual deficits.

Oral-Tactile Sensitivity Problems

As stated above, many clients with expressive speech and language disorders have oral-tactile sensitivity and tactile perceptual problems:

1. Hypersensitivity

Clients who are *hypersensitive* to oral-tactile experiences are described as being overly sensitive. They react to touch experiences on, in or around the mouth with pulling away, gagging, retracting the lips, closing the mouth tightly, turning the head, refusing or getting mad. Their reactions typically are strong, quick and decisive.

Children who are hypersensitive in the oral area typically limit the variety of foods they will eat by texture, temperature, smell and taste. They do not enjoy the sensations of tooth brushing and face washing, and their avoidance reaction is beyond that of the typical child who simply does not want to brush his teeth or wash his face.

These children gag very easily, and may gag when the lips or tip of the tongue is stimulated, or even when the shoulder or the chin is touched. Some gag upon presentation of a spoon in feeding or even when opening the mouth. As a result, children with oral-tactile hypersensitivity typically also avoid hand-to-mouth and object-to-mouth play.

Children with oral-tactile hypersensitivity also avoid playing with sound. As young children, they often limit the types of sounds with which they will experiment in vocal play and babbling. Later, these children sometimes actively avoid saying certain sounds — especially vibratory ones like raspberries and the voiced fricatives and affricates. Some of these children will allow sound to channel through the nose only and will not allow sound to vibrate through the mouth.

The client with oral-tactile hypersensitivity will avoid most experiences in which he perceives that someone wants to do something in or on his mouth. This includes the oral exam, oral prompting, motokinesthetic techniques and so forth. When told to "put your tongue up here," the hypersensitive child may refuse, switch topics, act shy or confused, or ignore you.

Children with oral-tactile hypersensitivity tend to hold their mouths in a "high guard" position, with the jaw and lips somewhat retracted and the tongue retracted and held high in the oral cavity. (Please see Stability and Mobility in Tongue Movement #2, Chapter Six for more information on this.) The high back positioning of the tongue results in distorted vowels and consonants, and backing may be their predominant deviant phonological pattern.

2. Hyposensitivity

Children who are *hyposensitive* to touch in, on and around the oral mechanism, on the other hand, typically enjoy oral-tactile experiences and may even crave them. These children LOVE to put things in the mouth. When eating, they tend to stuff the mouth entirely full but often are unable to manage the food and end up spitting some out. These children often do not recognize that they are making a huge mess with food all around their mouths, and they are usually unaware when food is left in the mouth after a meal.

The hyposensitive child often mouths toys and objects well beyond the time when it is appropriate for his age. He often develops oral sucking, chewing, licking and grinding habits.

The hyposensitive child often has co-occurring low oral tone, and may carry the mouth with the jaw slung low, the lips parted, and the tongue carried low and forward. Under these conditions, the tongue tends to move in gross, less well-differentiated movement patterns.

Children with oral-tactile hyposensitivity usually do not discriminate their oral touch experiences well, and, as a result, they have difficulty perceiving how sounds are made in the mouth, they do not remember them well, and they have difficulty figuring out how to make oral position changes. Oral movements tend to emerge slowly, and speech sound development typically is delayed.

3. Mixed Oral-Tactile Sensitivity

Some clients with speech disorder have mixed hyper- and hyposensitivity. Some parts of the mouth are over-sensitive while others are under-sensitive. For example, the outside of the mouth on the cheeks and lips may be hypersensitive while the inner-mouth cavity is hyposensitive. This pattern of mixed sensitivity may occur in the whole body as well.

4. Fluctuating Oral-Tactile Sensitivity

All of us have at least slightly fluctuating tactile sensitivity. Sometimes we like to be touched and other times we don't. Sometimes we want to curl up in a warm comforter or take a hot bath, and other times we like to be unencumbered.

Children with speech and language disorder and related oral-motor deficit sometimes have widely different responses to touch stimulation depending on their moods and emotional states. Sometimes they enjoy oral-tactile stimulation and other times they hate it! Wide fluctuations cause inconsistencies in a child's ability to make good oral-tactile judgements, and interfere with the child's oral-tactile discrimination and memory.

5. Tactile Defensiveness

The term *tactile defensiveness* has been used equally and interchangeably with the term "tactile hypersensitivity," however these terms do not mean the same thing. Tactile defensiveness is a term used to describe a strong negative, emotional and behavioral response to touch input.

Children with tactile defensive behavior do not like touch input and therefore withdraw from it, push it away, avoid it and react with strong negative emotion. Children with tactile defensive behavior can appear hypersensitive, however, they are not necessarily so. Tactile defensive behavior can occur whether a client is hypersensitive, hyposensitive or normal in tactile sensitivity.

Defensive behavior can be the result of a variety of things, for example, prior history of tactile sensitivity problems, physical or sexual abuse, feeding problems, chronic need for administering strong medications, and so forth. Each individual case needs to be assessed and causes of tactile defensive behavior need to be determined on a case-by-case basis. Treatment needs to be adjusted accordingly.

Examining Oral-Tactile Sensitivity

The examination of oral-tactile sensitivity consists of two parts: (1) examination of client history, and (2) direct assessment.

1. Case History

The case history is the first place where information about oral-tactile sensitivity is gained. It should include information about: (1) tooth brushing, (2) face washing, (3) eating habits, (4) food textures and temperatures eaten, (5) history of feeding needs through infancy, (6) prior diagnosis of oral-tactile problems, (7) prior diagnosis of whole-body tactile problems, (8) sensorimotor integrative status, (9) history of mouthing behavior, (10) history of vocal play, (11) history of oral habits, (12) history of oral injury, (13) history of tooth emergence, and (14) history of oral surgery.

The case history will reveal patterns of oral-tactile sensitivity. These patterns together with information gained from the direct assessment reveal problems in oral-tactile sensitivity.

2. Direct Assessment

The direct assessment of a client's oral-tactile sensitivity entails the application of hands-on procedures designed to determine the client's reaction to touch in and around the mouth. Light touch is used throughout the direct assessment since it is the most ticklish and irritating, and it will give the most clear responses. The direct assessment includes an evaluation of touch responses to at least: (A) the face and neck, (B) the lips, (C) the gums, (D) the inner cheek walls, (E) the hard palate, and (F) the posterior oral-pharyngeal area.

The goal of the oral-tactile assessment is to observe the client's reaction to touch in each part of the oral mechanism. Information gained from the case history should help shape and modify the assessment, however. For example, if the case history points to a clear pattern of tactile hypersensitivity, the direct assessment often is abandoned altogether and it is replaced immediately with activities designed to remediate the problem and normalize sensitivity.

A. The Face and Neck

- Stimulation: Apply light touch with hands, fingers or cloth to face and neck including the cheeks, nose, masseters, chin and under the chin.

- Normal Response: Child should tolerate stimulation easily and even enjoy sensations. A "ticklish" reaction should be expected.

- Hypersensitive Response: Child may not allow touch or may allow touch but show discomfort, pulling away, acting out, fear, facial grimace or lip retraction. In severe cases, the child may gag.

- Hyposensitive Response: Child may not realize he's being touched, may ignore touch, may show little or no reaction, or may "crave" more.

B. The Lips

- Stimulation: Apply light touch to upper lip, lower lip and both simultaneously with fingers or cloth.

- Normal Response: Child should tolerate stimulation easily and even enjoy sensations. A "ticklish" reaction should be expected.

• Hypersensitive Response: Child may not allow touch or may allow touch but show discomfort, pulling away, acting out, fear, facial grimace, or lip retraction. In severe cases, the child may gag.

• Hyposensitive Response: Child may not realize he's being touched, may show little or no reaction, or may "crave" more.

C. The Gums

• Stimulation: Place a Toothette or Ora-Swab on gum above upper central incisors. Stroke gum from midline to left and then from midline to right. Repeat on lower gums.

• Normal Response: Child should tolerate easily with no discomfort, however, may demonstrate "social reaction" to adult putting object in mouth.

• Hypersensitive Response: Child may not allow touch or may allow touch but show discomfort, pulling away, acting out, fear, facial grimace, or lip retraction. In severe cases, the child may gag.

• Hyposensitive Response: Child may not realize he's being touched; may show little or no reaction; may "crave" more stimulation; may withdraw from stimulation because he can't feel what is going on in the mouth.

D. The Inner Cheek Walls

• Stimulation: Do in conjunction with stimulation to gums described above. When the Toothette reaches back molar area on one side, stroke the inner cheek wall. Repeat on both sides.

• Normal Response: Child should tolerate easily with no discomfort, however, may demonstrate "social reaction" to adult putting object in mouth.

• Hypersensitive Response: Child may not allow touch or may allow touch but show discomfort, pulling away, acting out, fear, facial grimace, or lip retraction. In severe cases, the child may gag.

• Hyposensitive Response: Child may show little or no reaction, may "crave" more stimulation, or may withdraw because he can't fell what is going on in the mouth.

E. The Hard Palate

• Stimulation: Use Toothette or Ora-Swab to stroke hard palate.

• Normal Response: Child should be able to "barely tolerate" stimulation, show some aversive reaction such as pulling away, should demonstrate a "ticklish" response, and should try to "neutralize" sensations by rubbing tongue against palate.

• Hypersensitive Response: Child may not allow touch or may allow but show severe aversive reaction or gagging.

• Hyposensitive Response: Child may show little or no reaction, may "crave" more stimulation, or may withdraw because he can't feel what is going on in the mouth.

F. The Posterior Oral-Pharyngeal Area

Tactile stimulation to the posterior oral-pharyngeal area should elicit a gag response. The gag is a protective response which is present at birth, which reduces in strength at approximately eight months of age, but which persists into adulthood. It must be described in more detail than the five areas above because the gag is absolutely our best measure of intraoral tactile sensitivity.

We assess the gag in order to discover: (1) where it is set off, and (2) under what conditions it is set off. Response to the gag tells how well the client is processing incoming tactile sensations from articulatory contact in speech, feeding, and oral play. Response to gag stimulation helps us determine if the client is hyper- or hyposensitive in the oral-tactile system which, in turn, helps us determine our programming for oral-motor therapy.

Stimulation of the Gag: The gag can be stimulated in two basic ways:

1. Type 1 Stimulation: Stimulate the tongue by placing a tongue depressor, glycerine swab or toothette on the tongue tip and stroking down the midline from tip to back. The gag should be elicited at about the 2/3 point. The gag can be inhibited by many clients, therefore do not inform the client of your intent. Instead, "sneak" the gag stimulation into your process of assessing other areas of the oral-tactile mechanism.

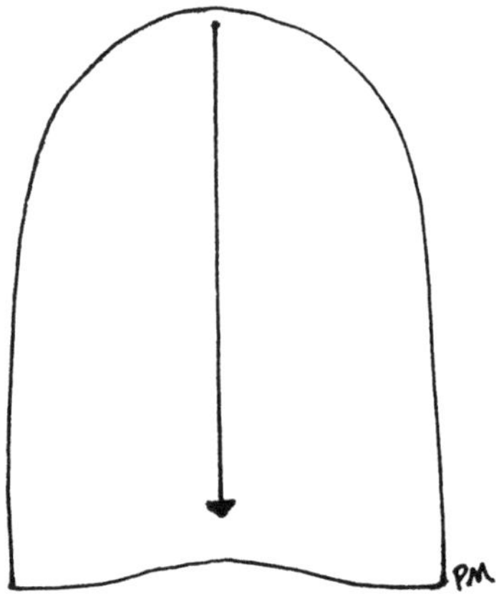

TYPE 1 STIMULATION

2. Type 2 Stimulation: Stimulate other oral structures. Touch the velum, soft palate or anterior faucial pillars. The gag is elicited at any one of these points. Again, do not inform your client of your intent.

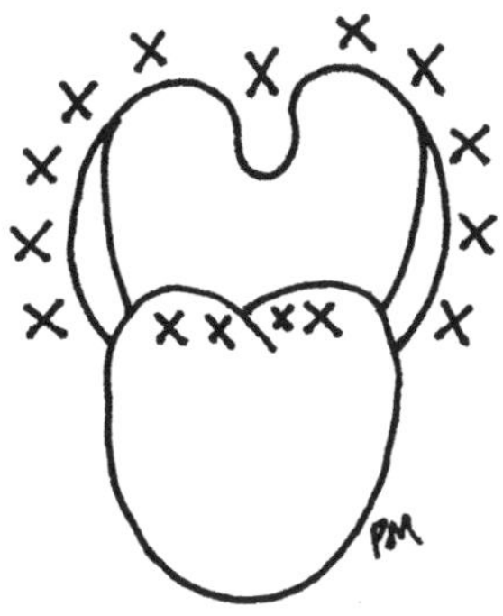

TYPE 2 STIMULATION

Follow Up: Since the gag is somewhat of an unpleasant sensation and can be somewhat scary to children, it is important to comfort the client after a gag is elicited. Say something like, “Oh, I'm sorry. That felt weird, didn't it?”

Response: The gag response has been described in various ways in different literature. Together the described characteristics of the gag bring us an overview of the full gag response:

1. The jaw moves downward and forward.
2. The tongue moves downward and forward.
3. The hyoid bone and larynx elevate.
4. The anterior and posterior faucial pillars move medially.
5. The velum elevates to protect the nasal airway.
6. The tongue takes on a predominate gutter shape with a deep midline fissure and high elevation of the lateral margins.

Children with oral-tactile sensitivity problems either over-respond or under-respond to stimulation of the gag.

Hypersensitivity: When the gag is hypersensitive, it is elicited anterior to the two-thirds position on the tongue. The gag may be elicited on the anterior half of the tongue or it may be elicited when the cheeks, lips or anterior gums are touched. The gag may even be elicited when the mouth is opened or when the upper body is touched.

A hypersensitive gag response over-rides any other responses the tongue and the rest of the oral mechanism could have to incoming touch experiences. Children who are hypersensitive in the oral area gag easily in oral motor play, feeding and some speech experiences. As a result they come to avoid these experiences. This denies the child the opportunity to respond normally to incoming oral exploratory play experiences which, in turn, can impede oral-motor development.

Sensitivity of the hypersensitive client needs to be normalized so that he can begin to respond more normally and with a full range of oral movement to incoming tactile and proprioceptive experiences in the mouth.

Hyposensitive: When the gag is hyposensitive to tactile stimulation in the mouth, the child perceives the incoming sensations less clearly and he is slower to respond. The gag may be absent, delayed or weak in response to either Type 1 or Type 2 stimulation. This child misses out on the oral-sensorimotor experiences necessary for good oral-motor development because he perceives them less well.

Sensitivity of the hyposensitive client needs to be normalized to improve oral-tactile awareness and discrimination.

Goals of Oral-Tactile Therapy

The good news about oral-tactile sensitivity problems is that most clients' responses can change over time with treatment. The following goals can be applied broadly to most clients:

1. To normalize the client's oral-tactile experiences.

2. To normalize the client's responses to oral-tactile input.

3. To increase awareness of the oral mechanism through touch experiences.

Notice the word "normalize" in goals one and two above. When a client's sensitivity level is high, we want to bring it down; when it is low, we want to bring it up. In either case, our therapy is aimed toward attaining a more "normal" experience.

Sometimes therapists make their oral-tactile goal for hypersensitive clients one of desensitizing a client to oral stimulation. THIS IS NOT AN APPROPRIATE GOAL. To desensitize a client to oral stimulation is to render him completely hyposensitive. This is not what we want. We want to bring the client to having rich oral-tactile experiences through oral-motor play, oral-motor learning and oral-motor stimulation with the result of increasing sensitivity and discriminatory abilities.

General Guidelines
For Normalizing Oral-Tactile Sensitivity

The following general guidelines for normalizing oral-tactile sensitivity describe concepts which interweave throughout the entire program.

1. Intrusion: We cannot intrude on a child's physical/tactile space quickly. We must move slowly in most cases.

2. Changes Over Time: Touch responses change moment-to-moment and day-to-day. The stimulation you provide will be changing the child's tactile responses. Therefore, he will change — sometimes within one session and other times after the session is over. Be mindful and watch for changes so that the stimulation you provide is always just what the child needs at the time.

3. Variations on the Body: Children often show variations in tactile sensitivity in different parts of their body. For example, a child may be hypersensitive extra-orally but hyposensitive intra-orally. Adjust your stimuli and your program accordingly.

4. Variations in Children: Every child is different. Therefore, we cannot employ one "cookbook" therapy program to reduce hypersensitivity. Instead, we must be creative therapists who follow our instincts and our background knowledge of the disorder.

5. Defensiveness: Watch carefully for signs of tactile defensiveness as they may be very subtle. Slight lip retraction, facial grimace, gag, choke, bite reflex, jaw thrust, jaw retraction, tongue retraction or slight turning of the head may be all you see.

6. Positioning: Correct positioning can facilitate more normal responses to tactile input.

7. Mouthing: These children often have been unable to engage in oral exploration or have avoided it. Once therapy to normalize sensitivity begins, they may begin oral self-exploratory play no matter their age. These behaviors should be viewed as normal responses to newly awakened oral sensations and management should be designed accordingly.

8. Teamwork: In the ideal situation, teamwork is best. Although only one therapist or parent may be doing the actual therapy, the team should at least include occupational and/or physical therapy, speech-language therapy and the parent or primary care-giver. All members of the team should be informed of the therapy program, its intent, and possible effects.

9. Also: Have fun, be safe, be flexible, be open to the child, take the primary care-giver's suggestions seriously, watch responses carefully as they may be subtle, and follow sanitary procedures throughout.

Stimulus Guidelines For Normalizing Oral-Tactile Sensitivity

The following stimulus guidelines present basic concepts about the type of stimuli used and client's reactions to them.

1. Surface Size: Broad surfaces of touch are usually tolerated more easily than smaller surfaces. Broad surfaces are more soothing, thus they are an excellent way to begin with the hypersensitive client.

2. Firmness: Firm touch is usually tolerated more easily than light touch. Firm touch is soothing, thus it is an excellent way to begin with the hypersensitive client.

3. Depth: Deep touch is usually tolerated more easily than light touch. Deep touch is soothing, thus it is an excellent way to begin with the hypersensitive client.

4. Touch-Release: Touch with immediate release may be tolerated more easily than touch which is maintained. It may be tolerated more easily by the hypersensitive child. However, sometimes maintaining touch may help the child "break through" a fearful response.

5. Movement: Stationary touch may be tolerated more easily than moving (stroking) touch, thus it may be tolerated more easily by the hypersensitive child. However, some programs advocate the use of "forced stroking." Forced stroking has been found to be a powerful means of bringing down sensitivity level quickly; however, its powerful effect on the arousal system requires that it be administered by therapists highly trained in sensorimotor integrative therapy.

6. Stroking: Stroking with the grain of hairs is soothing and calming and may be tolerated more easily by the hypersensitive child. Stroking against the grain of hairs is irritating and can be used to excite and increase activity level.

7. Cold Temperatures: Cold stimulation may be tolerated easily and may help the client tolerate touch to parts he otherwise wouldn't or can't. Use: ice, cold food, a cold wet washcloth or cold hands.

8. Warm Temperatures: Heat may also help as in #7 above. Use: a dry washcloth or blanket, warm food, warm hands, warm water bottle or a heating pad.

9. Vibration: Vibration may help organize touch perceptions or may be hated and rejected! Vibrations differ by frequency and amplitude, and may be applied manually or with a battery-operated or electrical vibrator. Consult your team OT/PT for specifics and advice. Do not use vibration with children with neurological impairment or seizure disorders without prior OT/PT/Neurological consult and team decision-making. Use vibration first under the direction of someone who knows how to use it.

10. Source of Touch: Touch the child applies to himself (e.g., child puts his own finger in mouth), touch with which the child is very familiar (e.g., nightly tooth brushing), and touch over which the child has control (e.g., allowing the child to stimulate himself). These are the easiest to tolerate and may be accepted more readily by the hypersensitive child.

11. Food: Food snacks with which the client is familiar usually are the most readily accepted forms of interoral tactile stimulation. Use food to work in the mouth when the client is hyposensitive in the mouth but hypersensitive outside of it.

12. Visual Feedback: Visual feedback (use of a mirror) often aids the child's perceptions of incoming tactile sensations and may help improve tolerance.

Organizational Guidelines For Normalizing Oral-Tactile Sensitivity

The following organizational guidelines present the overall approach to treatment.

1. Avoid Negative Responses: Maintain your touch stimuli until you feel that you are about to see an aversive reaction or until you see one that couldn't be avoided. You are trying to provide an environment in which the child feels safe with the stimulation that you are supplying him, and thus you want to avoid aversive responses. When you get one, this means that you must change your stimulus according to the Stimulus Guidelines given above.

2. Work from Least-to-Most Sensitive: Work from the least sensitive parts of the body to the most sensitive ones. The oral area, including the neck and shoulders, often is the most sensitive part of the entire body. Thus, sometimes you must work from the hands and feet to the trunk and eventually to the head, face and mouth. Watch out, however, because sometimes the hands and feet are the most sensitive areas.

3. Work Extra-Oral to Intra-Oral: In general, you will want to work from extraoral to intraoral. Work from the whole body to the head, face, ears, cheeks, entire mouth region, lips, gums, tongue and palate, roughly in that order. However, be very aware that some children are more sensitive outside the mouth than they are inside the mouth. Thus, with them you will want to go directly into the mouth and work your way out. Use food snacks for this.

4. Work the Mouth: When you begin to work inside the mouth, consider working the whole inner surface first by stuffing the mouth with appropriate items. Then work the gums. Stroke the upper gum from midline to the back at one molar area. Return to midline and work back to the molar area on the opposite side. Repeat for the lower gums. Stimulate the inner cheek walls during this time.

5. Work the Tongue: In working the tongue, begin with stimulation to the entire upper surface of the tongue, then the tip and down the midline to the back. Watch carefully for the gag reflex — its presence indicates that the child is not tolerating your input and thus you must make some adjustments. You want to structure your therapy so that the gag is used as a tolerance indicator. If it is elicited too far anterior to normal, work so that the child gradually tolerates more and varied tactile input before the gag is elicited.

6. Be Verbally Explicit: Label and describe everything that you are doing to the child as it happens and describe every response that the child has. This aids top-down processing. For example, in preparation for stimulation say, "Now I'm going to touch your lips." During stimulation say, "I'm touching your lips." After a positive reaction to stimulation say, "Hey. You let me touch your lips." After a negative reaction say, "That felt awful, didn't it?"

The Proprioception System

The term proprioception refers to sensations which arise from muscles and joints. Our muscles give us information about their state of contraction or relaxation, the rate at which they are contracting or relaxing, and the degree to which the contraction and relaxation occurs. This data is organized and used to perceive the position our body is in and the way in which it is moving in relationship to itself.

Our joints give us information about the physical relationship of one bone as it articulates with another bone. Neurological receptors in a joint send information to the brain regarding: (1) the state of bending or straightening, (2) the rate of bending or straightening, (3) the degree of bending or straightening, and (4) the degree of rotation in a joint.

We depend to a much lesser extent on proprioceptive information than we do on tactile information as a means of monitoring oral movements. Thus proprioceptive stimulation is used less to teach oral position and more to stimulate muscles and joints in order to adjust muscular tone and reactivity, and to give the client more information about and awareness of the parts of the oral mechanism.

Proprioceptive Stimulation Techniques

Hands-on oral proprioceptive stimulation is used in oral-motor therapy to improve general oral-motor abilities as well as to facilitate specific oral-motor responses. The following describes how muscles respond to proprioceptive stimulation. Please note that how the technique is applied determines how muscles will react to it.

1. Stretching Muscles: Quick stretching to a muscle sends excitatory messages to it and inhibitory messages to its antagonist. The faster the stretch is applied (quick

stretch), the more facilitory it will be. Slow stretching, on the other hand, is relaxing to a muscle. Many massage techniques are based in slowly stretching muscles along their length.

2. Resisting Movement: Resistance is applied in the opposite direction to which a client is purposefully moving a body part in order to increase the effort which is required. Resistance adds weight to oral movement, and it will help increase the range of movement. Resistance is one of the most useful tools in oral-motor therapy. Repetition of movement under resistance is used to develop skill, strength and endurance. We do not "resist" uncoordinated or undesired movements as this will increase and strengthen them.

3. Compressing Joints: Compressing, or approximating, a joint has two different effects depending upon the force used: (a) joint compression of body weight or less inhibits hypertonic muscles around a joint, and (b) joint compression of more than body weight facilitates co-contraction at the joint. The only joint in the oral mechanism is the temporomandibular joint. WE DO NOT USE COMPRESSION IN ORAL-MOTOR THERAPY BECAUSE WE DO NOT WANT TO DAMAGE THE TEMPOROMANDIBULAR JOINT.

4. Drawing on Joints: Traction, or drawing on a body part, stimulates the joint receptors and thus stimulates the muscles around the joint into pulling. The only joint in the oral mechanism is the temporomandibular joint. WE DO NOT USE TRACTION IN ORAL-MOTOR THERAPY BECAUSE WE DO NOT WANT TO DAMAGE THE TEMPOROMANDIBULAR JOINT.

5. Vibrating Skin and Underlying Muscles: Vibration actually derives from touch and artificially stimulates the muscles underlying the skin. Slow manual vibration can help relax oral muscles. Quick vibration "wakes up!" the oral mechanism, draws the child's attention to it and increases overall tone.

6. Pressing and Tapping: Brief intermittent pressure or tapping to a muscle belly is facilitory. Pressure to a muscle belly followed by stretch of the muscle towards both ends is facilitory. Pressure to the point of insertion of a muscle is inhibitory.

Oral Exploratory Play For Hands-Off Oral-Motor Learning

What we have described up to this point has been hands-on tactile and proprioceptive stimulation techniques. Oral exploratory play (OEP) is a process of engaging in hands-off oral-motor learning. Oral exploratory play is the process of encouraging the child's own self-exploration of his own oral mechanism, and it is an attempt to help the client recreate the process of mouthing play seen in the infant and toddler. It helps normalize oral-tactile sensitivity and it helps children learn new oral movements. OEP is preferable in most cases, and it can be combined with hands-on methods.

For oral exploratory play, one needs: (1) visual input in the form of mirrors, pictures, models and so forth, (2) auditory input in the form of slight amplification, auditory models and verbal descriptions, (3) oral-tactile input in the form of food, drink, ice, Toothettes, horns, whistles, kazoos, tubes, etc., and (4) oral-proprioceptive input in the form of pressure, tapping, stretching and so forth.

During OEP, the therapist allows the child to explore his mouth on his own — what it feels like, what it does, how it moves and so forth. The therapist imitates what the child does and describes it to him in terms he can understand to make the process salient to him.

Therapists use comments, questions and suggestions to encourage the child. Therapy goals are to help clients: (1) to explore with a greater number and variety of tools and toys, (2) to spend increasingly longer periods of time exploring, (3) to make a greater number and variety of oral movements during his explorations, and (4) to make a greater number and variety of sounds during this time.

OEP can be incorporated into individual or group speech and language therapy sessions, or into classroom activities, and it also can be done at home. OEP can be done from five minutes to one hour, depending upon the client's interest and skill level.

OEP allows a child to become more aware of his own oral abilities. It encourages him to do more of what he can do and to learn new oral movements. It helps him pay attention to you and what you can do with your mouth. It helps develop auditory-visual-tactile organization around mouth movements, it facilitates the development of early oral-motor imitation skill, and it facilitates the emergence of vocalizations and speech sounds.

S.A.T.P.I.O.M.'s

Items to be used in oral-motor therapy and OEP must be carefully selected. Toward this end, the concept of using Socially-Appropriate Things to Put In and On the Mouth (S.A.T.P.I.O.M.'s) has been designed.

S.A.T.P.I.O.M.'s meet certain criteria. They are items which are: (1) socially appropriate, (2) sanitary, (3) safe, and (4) inexpensive. For example, a toothbrush meets all four criteria. Toothbrushes are easy to come by, can be purchased in bulk for reduced cost, are very familiar to clients, and can be cleaned and sanitized.

S.A.T.P.I.O.M.'s in common use today include:

Toothbrushes	Toothettes	Dental Floss
Horns	Whistles	Sirens
Harmonicas	Straws	Tubes
Ora-Swabs	Glycerine Swabs	Lip Retractors
Bubble Blowers	Rubber Tubing	Vinyl Tubing
Megaphones	Plastic Microphones	Tongue Depressors
Bitesticks	Lollipop Sticks	Paper Towel Tubes
Toy Food	Balloons	Inspiration Spirometers
Nuk Massage Brushes	Baby Teething Toys	Doggie Chew Toys
Party Favors	Theraspoons	Plastic Spoons
Baby Spoons	Pacifiers	Adult-Size Pacifiers
Wash Cloths	Infadent Toothbrushes	Rubber Balls
Dental Floss Holders	Lip Gyms	Nasal Clamps
Laryngeal Mirrors	Vibrators	Flavored Tongue Depressors
Bite Blocks	Nasal Flutes	Cocktail Straws

New products that can be used for oral stimulation and oral exploratory play are arriving on the market daily. Therapists are urged to keep an eye out for new items in the areas of dental care, infant feeding and teething, pet chewing, oral cleaning and so forth.

S.A.T.P.I.O.M.'s also include food. The following types are common in therapy use:

- Small Dry Snacks: small crackers, small cookies, pretzels, etc.
- Purees: puddings, applesauce, yogurt, etc.
- Cold Foods: ice, Popsicles, ice cream, etc.
- Tiny Candies: cake decorations, chocolate chips, etc.
- Tiny Foods: raisins, dried cranberries, bits of apple, etc.
- Chewy Foods: licorice, dried fruit, etc.
- Thick and Thin Liquids: water, juice, milk shakes, etc.

Sample Procedures
To Improve Oral-Tactile Sensitivity

These sample activities designed to help improve oral-tactile sensitivity are provided to help the reader begin to understand how to do oral-motor activities in oral exploratory play. Each activity is described for one young child; adaptations for groups and older children must be made.

1. Use Oral Toys: Use horns, whistles, kazoos, sirens, harmonicas, blow toys, inspiration spirometers, infant teething toys and plastic food as tools in therapy. Allow the client to explore each toy, and show him how to use it.

• Effects: Toys help motivate a client to put things into the mouth in a socially appropriate way, and since they are non-threatening, children typically will play with them for a long time. Blow toys, of course, enhance inhalation and exhalation capability, as well as improve oral (jaw, lip, tongue) awareness, movements and control. Work toward increasing the length of time the client will engage with the toys and the types of oral movements he does with them.

2. Use Oral Tools: Use Toothettes, tongue depressors, spoons, bitesticks, craft sticks, straws, rubber or vinyl tubing, plastic pipes, toothbrushes, dental floss, dental floss holders and other "tools" to explore the mouth. Brush the teeth, explore the mouth, make sound in and on the objects, and so forth.

• Effects: Tools help motivate a client to put things into the mouth in a socially appropriate way. Most are non-threatening and children typically will play with them for a long time. Work toward increasing the length of time the client will engage with the tools, and the number and variety of actions he performs with them.

3. Label Objects and Actions: As you work through your oral-motor program, label and describe the toys and tools, the things you do with them, the body parts touched in the process, the emotional responses you perceive that the child has to them, and the child's oral movement responses. For example, as the child is using a harmonica, say over time:

"That goes in your mouth..."
"Can you blow it?..."
"You can suck it too..."
"Your tongue tip can fit in the tiny holes..."
"You can bite on it to hold it without your hands..."
"This one is bigger than that one. Can you get it in your mouth too?..."
"Your teeth are showing..."
"Press your lips on it..."

• Effects: By labeling body parts and actions, children begin to understand and use language to organize what has heretofore been unorganized or unclear. Label the body parts in minute detail according to the child's level of understanding.

4. Use Ice Cubes: Fill 2-oz. paper cups half-full of water and keep a half-dozen or so in the freezer. Sit the child down in front of a mirror, peel back the top of one paper cup so that the ice is exposed, and let him play with it. Use one yourself to demonstrate fun things to do with it if the child is stuck or to get him going. Suck them, blow on them, blow raspberries on them, vocalize on them, lick them, pocket them in the mouth and so forth.

Ice cubes can be used almost any time at home as a snack, and they're a nice reinforcer to use during other oral-motor or articulation therapy activities. Let the child suck the cube for 15-30 seconds between turns or drills.

• Effects: When used for short periods of time, cold stimuli decreases sensitivity in most cases of over-sensitivity, and increases sensitivity in most cases of under-sensitivity. Cold temperatures also help increase muscle tone when employed for a short period of time. After that, muscle tone relaxes. To achieve maximum benefit from ice in order to increase tonus, allow the child to suck the ice for no more than 30 seconds at a time during a 10-minute interval. Improved tonus through cold stimulation will improve overall oral movements. After that, range and speed of oral movement will decrease.

5. Use Dry or Wet Wash Cloths: Ask parents to bring a terry wash cloth to therapy that can be left in a container in the room to use in many ways. Provide it for the child to use in many ways: (A) use the washcloth to "get" the child's lips, tongue, cheeks, etc.; (B) encourage the child to pretend to be any number of animals and hold the washcloth with his mouth, either by the teeth or the lips — chew on the washcloth, shake it, tug on it, make animal sounds with it in the mouth; (C) as the child holds the washcloth in his mouth, gently tug on it, tease and say, "Give me that towel!"; (D) pretend to wash the face to the tune of "This is the way we wash our face, wash our face, wash our face. This is the way we wash our face so early in the morning."

• Effects: These are wonderful activities to improve oral-tactile awareness and gross tactile discrimination of the face, lips, gums, tongue and palate. The more towel in the mouth, the more skin surface is stimulated. Use of various temperatures or wet/dry differences also helps the child with gross oral discrimination. Gentle tugging of the cloth while it is held in the mouth by the lips provides excellent stimulus to help strengthen the lip and facial muscles. Gentle tugging when held by the teeth gives the masseters and temporomandibular joint proprioceptive stimulation.

6. Play "Peek-a-Boo": Use towels and blankets of various weights and textures to play "Peek-a-Boo." When the cloth is over your head, encourage the child to feel the parts of your face and head with his hands. When the cloth is over the child's head, use this opportunity to give gross tactile input with your hands to the facial structures. Encourage the child to touch his or her own face in this way.

• Effects: This is an excellent way to give gross firm and light touch stimuli to the entire head and face as a preliminary step to more discrete oral stimulation. Hiding under a blanket can help a hypersensitive client feel more safe.

7. Use Gooey Food for Oral Play: Provide the child with a serving tray or large piece of waxed paper to serve as a place setting. Plop down a substantial scoop of prepared pudding. Encourage the child to explore the pudding with his clean hands and fingers. Let the child lick his hands and fingers at will.

• Effects: This activity is designed, of course, to encourage hand-to-mouth play.

Oral-tactile awareness, discrimination and localization are stimulated. (WARNING: Do not follow this activity with regular finger painting!!)

8. Use Toothbrushes and Toothettes: Use toothbrushes and Toothettes to pretend to brush the teeth and to explore the interoral cavity.

- Effects: Toothbrushes are a natural way to provide a strong stimulus to the oral cavity. Toothettes are softer after they become wet with saliva and are thus less powerful. Using a toothbrush is something that most children are already familiar with. Use adult brushes, small child-size brushes, and brushes with all or most of the bristles shaved off for variety in textural experiences.

9. Eat Dry Snacks: Provide the child with a dry snack, such as crackers, to eat while watching in a mirror. Encourage the child to watch himself eat. Model exaggerated chewing. Encourage the child to open the mouth to discover the chewing and swallowing process. Comment about the sloppy texture of the food. Model exaggerated swallowing. Check the mouth to see if all the tiny mashed bits have been swallowed.

Many of our clients leave a substantial amount of food in the mouth and do not completely evacuate when swallowing. Poke fun at this and say, "Swallow more. You have to swallow more to get all the food down." Encourage the child to make broad sweeps of the tongue all throughout the mouth to clear it and to swallow more. Continue to check for an empty mouth. When the mouth is as completely evacuated as you believe the child is capable at the time, allow a second cracker. Best snack foods: Fish Crackers and Animal Cookies.

- Effects: The tactile experience of food in the mouth is the easiest, most natural way to give interoral-tactile stimulation. You are trying to bring conscious awareness to the act of eating — what it feels like, what the jaw can do, what the tongue can do, how to clear the mouth, what swallowing is, and so forth. This activity will stimulate the child to become more aware of the oral-tactile experience every time he eats. Thus, a large part of your work will be reinforced at home during every snack and meal. Eating is a great activity for "food-stuffers" since it brings into focus the tactile sensations that the child seeks when he stuffs his mouth full. It teaches him how to take individual small bites, and it teaches him to completely evacuate the mouth when swallowing.

Chapter Three Summary

Chapter Three has presented an overview of the tactile and proprioceptive systems and their relationship to articulation and phonological therapy. Tactile abilities and problems in oral-tactile sensitivity have been discussed, as have goals, guidelines and methods for assessment and treatment. The process of oral-exploratory play for hands-off oral-motor learning using socially-appropriate items has been presented. Proprioceptive stimulation techniques to influence muscle tone and reactivity have also been introduced.

Chapter 4

The Jaw

Chapter Contents

1. Jaw Movements
2. Jaw Movements in Mature Speech
3. Jaw Movements in Development
4. The Jaw-Tongue-Palate Triangle
5. Diagnosing Jaw Movements
6. Deviations in Jaw Movements
7. Jaw Facilitation Techniques

In this chapter we begin a discussion of how tactile and proprioceptive stimulation techniques can be used to facilitate specific jaw, lip and tongue movements. In this chapter our focus is on the jaw.

Although the jaw and its movements have been virtually ignored in the articulation and phonological literature, the jaw is the most fundamental moving oral part from an oral-motor perspective. The jaw is the "house" for the lips and tongue: it is the bone and hard tissue against which the soft tissues of lips and tongue function.

The jaw is the earliest part of the oral mechanism to function in development. Gross jaw movements are the ones that get the entire oral mechanism to begin moving, and its development determines maturation level of lip and tongue movements. If the jaw doesn't move, the lips and tongue probably don't either; if the jaw deviates in its movements, the lips and tongue probably do as well.

In this chapter we shall discuss: (1) jaw movements in mature speech and in speech development, (2) the diagnosis of jaw movements, (3) deviations in jaw movements which are common in the speech impaired population, and (4) techniques to facilitate improved jaw movements for speech.

Jaw Movements

The jaw is a bone which hangs below the head and articulates with it at the temporomandibular joint (TMJ). Because the TMJ is a ball-and-socket joint, the jaw is free to move in the following directions: (1) up and down, (2) left and right, (3) forward and back, and (4) in rotation in all directions.

Jaw Movements in Mature Speech

The jaw moves in finely graded patterns in mature speech:

1. Up and Down

The jaw moves up and down during rapid mature conversational speech in a restricted yet visible range of finely graded up and down positions. It can move down into a fully-open mouth position, and it can close tightly into a clench, but it does neither in the course of everyday conversational speech.

2. Left and Right

The jaw moves left and right in rapid mature conversational speech in very finely graded movement patterns that are, for all practical purposes, invisible to the naked eye. It can swing widely left and widely right, but it does neither in the course of everyday conversational speech.

3. Forward and Back

The jaw moves forward and back in very finely graded movement patterns during mature rapid conversational speech. The amount of forward movement is related to the distance between the upper and lower incisors. When the gap between the upper and lower incisors is wide, the jaw moves forward for the teeth to meet for production of sibilants. The jaw can push forward substantially and retract stiffly backward, but it does neither in the course of everyday conversational speech.

4. Rotary

In mature speech, the jaw moves in rotary patterns in all directions. These are slight and very finely graded, so much so that they are invisible to the naked eye for all practical purposes. Again, the jaw can rotate in big movement patterns in all directions, but it does not do so in the course of everyday conversational speech.

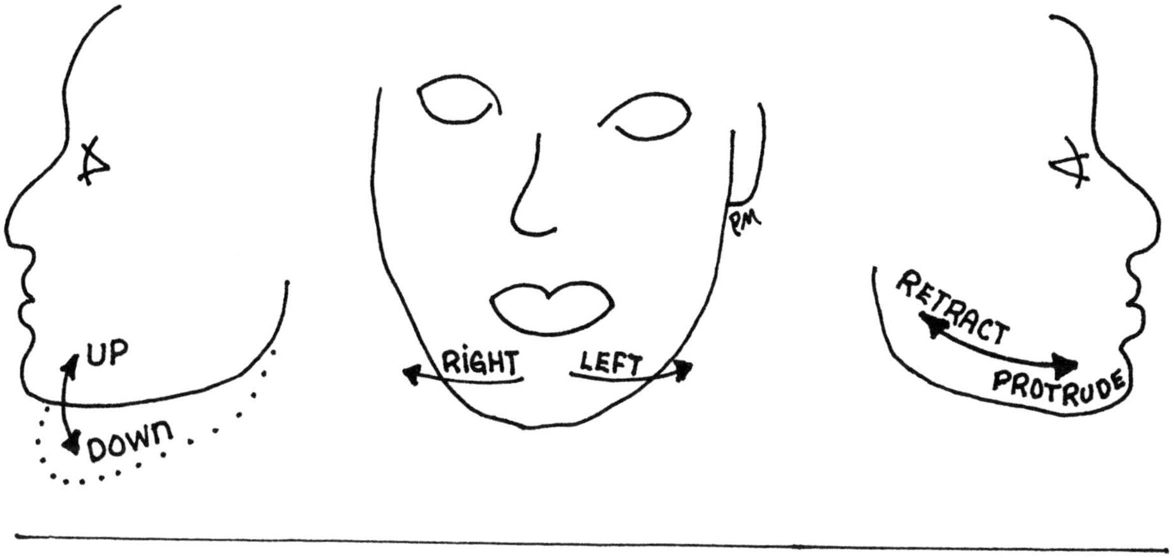

JAW MOVEMENTS

Jaw Movements in Development

The jaw's developmental movement patterns reflect all the principles of movement outlined in our second chapter. However, the most useful principle for understanding jaw movements in speech regards the process of developing movement from gross to fine.

The jaw begins its journey of development in big, gross movement patterns. All jaw movements — up/down, left/right, forward/back and rotary — move in big patterns early in development and in smaller more refined and finely graded patterns over time.

This developmental sequence is reflected in speech. For example, early babbling sequences are produced with big up and down movements of the jaw. Over time, the jaw gradually moves into increasingly smaller or more finely graded up-and-down movement patterns. This allows the lips and tongue to take over more of the work.

In general, while the jaw moves in large immature patterns, the lips and tongue move less. As the jaw's movements become more restricted, the lips and tongue become more active.

Jaw movements also are a catalyst for early lip and tongue movement. For example, as the jaw begins to move left-and-right, the tongue is carried with it. Over time, the tongue begins to differentiate its movements from that of the jaw and moves left and right all by itself.

The Jaw-Tongue-Palate Triangle

The jaw, tongue and palate together form a three-part movement unit with each part moving independently from the others yet together in a coordinated fashion. To understand this three-part relationship, it helps to think of the tongue and palate as being two partners in a marriage, with the jaw being an outside third party that can support or detract from the marriage.

For the advanced production of speech, the tongue and palate are intimately intertwined. The tongue lifts and lowers its itself toward and against the palate for production of all the lingua phonemes. As long as the tongue is situated immediately below the palate, it can lift its component parts to articulate with the palate in just the right way and in the right place.

The jaw, being the third party and being the "house" for the tongue, effects their marriage with its every move. The jaw literally carries the tongue, and the way it moves influences the tongue's movements and the tongue's relationship to the palate.

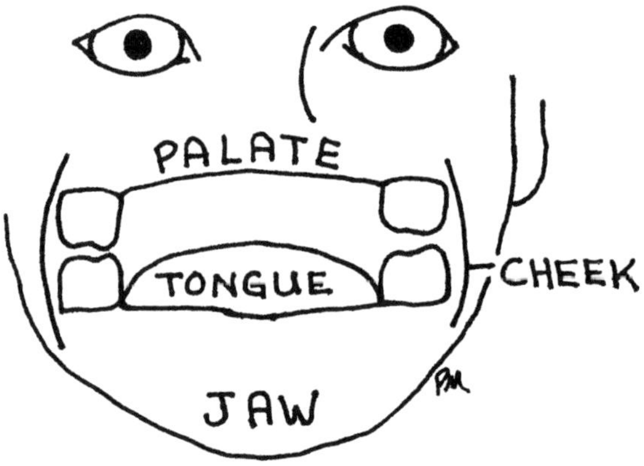

JAW-TONGUE-PALATE TRIANGLE

For example, if the jaw moves too far left during speech, the tongue will be carried with it and place of articulation on the palate will change. If the tongue is to articulate correctly, it will have to compensate for the jaw's excessive movement pattern.

This type of movement compensation on the part of the tongue can be done by a mature speaker; however, it cannot be and is not done in early development. Thus, if the jaw moves inappropriately in oral-motor development, the tongue will learn incorrect movement patterns. Together, inappropriate jaw and tongue movement patterns make for incorrect articulation. Facilitation of correct jaw movements, therefore, is critical for the development of appropriate tongue movements in speech.

Diagnosing Jaw Movements

To diagnose jaw movements, observe them: (1) at rest, (2) in spontaneous and imitated speech tasks, (3) in oral motor imitation tasks, and (4) in feeding.

1. Rest Posture: Observe the position and movements of the jaw when the child's mouth is at rest — meaning that he is not involved in speech, feeding or oral-motor play behavior. The jaw should be held slightly downward so that the teeth are not meeting.

2. Articulation Testing: Note the position and movement of the jaw during connected speech and during articulation testing. The jaw should move in finely graded movement patterns as described above in mature speech.

3. Oral-Motor Exam and Imitation Tasks: Observe jaw function during the oral exam and during oral-motor imitation tasks. Also, observe jaw movements during the assessment of tactile stimulation, and note how the jaw functions before, during and after this stimulation. The mature speaker should be able to move the jaw voluntarily in all directions.

4. Feeding: Observe the jaw while the child is eating and drinking. Note differences in jaw mobility when the child is eating foods of various thickness, textures and wetness. Note the position of the jaw during cup-drinking, biting, chewing, food transfer, swallowing and lip cleaning. Deeper knowledge of feeding development will aid this aspect of the analysis.

5. Consultation with Motor Therapists: A complete assessment of jaw mobility should be concluded with consultation from motor specialists when a client has a pervasive neuromuscular disorder or fine and gross motor delay. These team members can identify problems in overall tactile sensitivity, tone, reflexes, balance, and hip, shoulder, neck and head position which can help with a thorough assessment of the causes of the client's jaw movement problems.

Deviations in Jaw Movements

Children with articulation and phonological delay or disorder and related oral-motor dysfunction can have one or more of the following deviant jaw movement patterns:

1. Restricted Movement: As stated above, early in development the jaw moves a great deal and in doing so stimulates the tongue and lips to move. This is a necessary step in oral-motor development. When the jaw is restricted in its movements, it does not move enough for speech to emerge correctly. The client will be unable to open the mouth far, will be unable to clench the jaw for strong biting and chewing, and will not lateralize, protrude, retract or move in rotation as maturation should allow. Therapy needs to be directed toward increasing range of jaw movement.

2. Excessive Up-and-Down Movements: Excessive up-and-down movement is an indication that oral movements are delayed and are moving more grossly. When the jaw moves grossly, the tongue and lips will be delayed in their movements. Therapy needs to be directed toward increasing jaw stability after it has achieved maximum mobility.

3. Excessive Lateralization: Excessive lateralization of the jaw in speech can be related to muscle tone disturbance. When tone is low, the jaw lateralizes because it is slung too loosely. In this case, treatment is directed toward increasing tone and stabilizing the jaw at midline. When tone is high, the jaw pulls strongly to the side of higher tone. In this case, treatment is directed toward decreasing overall tone, increasing jaw flexibility and stabilizing the jaw at midline.

4. Excessive Protrusion: Jaw protrusion is defined as forward movement of the jaw so that the lower incisors become positioned anterior to the upper incisors. Excessive protrusion of the jaw draws the tongue forward with it, causing a frontal lisping pattern. This is not interdental lisping, however, and is not a problem with the tongue — it is a problem of the jaw. Jaw protrusion needs to be carefully diagnosed to differentiate it from a structural problem. Structural problems need to be addressed by medical and/or orthodontic professionals. Excessive protrusion which is an oral-motor problem necessitates treatment directed toward stabilizing the jaw in a more posterior correct position.

5. Excessive Retraction: Excessive retraction often is an indication of oral-tactile hypersensitivity and can be part of an overall pattern of jaw-lip-tongue-head retraction. Muscle tone problems usually are a cause. Therapy is directed toward: (1) normalizing oral-tactile sensitivity, (2) normalizing overall tone, (3) inhibiting abnormal upper body movement patterns and (4) facilitating more normal ones.

6. Jerky Movements: Jerkiness when the jaw moves is an indication of poor movement gradation. Instead of smoothly moving the jaw, the client jerks it into place. Muscle tone problems are likely. Treatment is directed toward: (1) normalizing overall oral tone, (2) learning to move the jaw in smaller ranges of movement, and (3) moving the jaw more rhythmically and smoothly.

7. Combinations: Any combinations of the above named problems can occur with speech impairment. Treatment is directed toward a combination of the above approaches.

Jaw Facilitation Techniques

Jaw facilitation techniques are found in the feeding therapy, the motor therapy, the dysphagia therapy, and the myofunctional therapy literature. They are designed to: (1) increase awareness of the jaw as a moving oral part, (2) increase range of jaw movement and jaw mobility, (3) develop jaw stability, (4) increase strength of the bite and chew, (5) increase endurance for moving the jaw, and (6) develop a finely graded open position for speech.

1. Oral Control — Developing Oral Awareness

Oral control (earlier termed jaw control) can be used to develop jaw stability and jaw mobility. Hands-on techniques are used to get the jaw to move and to inhibit excessive or inappropriate jaw movements. By facilitating improved jaw control, we give the child the foundation for learning advanced lip and tongue movements. Hands-off techniques are used by the child to learn and monitor jaw movements.

Depending upon which technique is used, oral control: (1) adds weight, (2) increases awareness of the jaw and its movements, (3) increases strength of masseter control, (4) gives external stability to the jaw, and (5) helps reduce jaw movements.

A. Side Control: Side control is a hands-on technique. Sit beside or slightly behind the child. Shape your hand in a traditional "two" posture. Reach around behind the child with your arm and take hold of the jaw with your fingers by placing your middle finger under the child's chin (used to help keep the jaw closed and the tongue in), and your index finger on the front of the chin itself (used to help the jaw open and move the lower lip). Your fingers should lie flat, i.e., don't use just the tips. Let the child rest the back of the head against your upper arm. Pull slightly upward on the head and jaw to pull the head gently into a good upright position. Use to hold the jaw in a stable position and to move the jaw.

B. Front Control: Front control is a hands-on technique. Sit in front of the child and place your thumb tip on the front of the chin (assists in jaw opening), place your bent index finger under the chin (assists with jaw closure.) Use to hold the jaw in a stable position and to move the jaw.

C. Self Monitoring: Self monitoring is a hands-off technique. Have the child hold his own jaw to discover and monitor its movements:

1. Palming Method: Place the palms of the hands on the jaw with the heal of the hand on the chin and the fingertips on the TMJ. Use to help increase jaw awareness and to encourage increased mobility.

2. Fingertip Method: Place the fingertips on the TMJ and the thumb tip on the tip of the chin. Use to monitor and voluntarily reduce jaw movements.

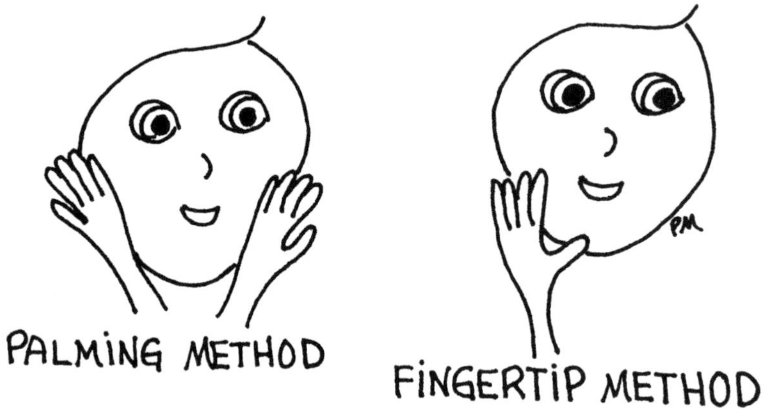

2. Jaw Resistance — Developing Mobility and Stability

Jaw resistance is the easiest and most effective technique we can use to improve internal jaw stability and mobility. It entails purposeful movement control by the client as the stimulus is being applied. It is used to increase jaw strength and range of movement.

We use oral control positions (see above) to resist or oppose the direction that the jaw is purposefully and voluntarily being moved in order to maximize the effort required. "Resist" does not mean "prevent" — it means to make the movement a little more effortful. We can resist jaw movements in all directions, however, resistance to up-and-down movements has the most far-reaching effects on jaw mobility.

Resisting jaw movements: (1) adds weights to the jaw, (2) increases range of motion of jaw movements, (3) increases awareness of jaw movements, (4) increases strength of the masseters, and (5) increases endurance for increasingly complex speech, feeding, and oral-motor tasks.

A. Lowering: This is a hands-on technique. To resist jaw-lowering (mouth opening), place your fingers in Front Jaw Control position and push the chin gently but firmly upwards with your index finger as the child attempts to move the jaw down (open the mouth).

B. Elevating: This is a hands-on technique. To resist jaw elevation (mouth closing), place your fingers in Front Jaw Control position and push the chin gently but firmly down with your thumb as the child attempts to move the jaw up (close the mouth).

C. Sequencing: This is a hands-on technique. A combination of the techniques given in A and B above can be used to facilitate better sequential movements. Therapists are urged to work in these sequences only after becoming somewhat proficient in applying each technique individually. To use the techniques in sequence, simply apply one and then the other in smooth and increasingly rapid sequences as the client opens and closes the mouth.

D. Chewing: Chewing on foods and appropriate oral chew toys and tools of increasing resilience is a highly effective resistance technique which is hands-off. Use infant teething toys, vinyl or rubber tubing, or toy food. Sort the toys and tools by firmness, and present them from soft to firm. Strength will increase as the child develops the ability to chew items of increasing firmness.

3. Objects — Developing External Stability

Using external stability is a process of bracing a body part against another body part or against an object. The process of external stability is a very easy yet effective way to stabilize the jaw since it stabilizes the jaw in a partially-open position, is non-invasive and allows for self-control on the part of the child. We stabilize the jaw by biting down on objects. Bite down at the molars on both sides simultaneously, or on one side and then the other.

A. Large Objects: By biting down on a wide or large firm object, one can stabilize the jaw in a lowered position to prop the mouth open wide. This is an excellent position from which to practice large lip and tongue movements, and to rehearse some speech. Bite at the molars on: firm infant chew toys, firm plastic food, tongue depressors seated sideways, a large bite block, and so forth.

B. Small Objects: Narrow objects stabilize the jaw high so that the mouth is propped in a more narrow or partially open position. This is an excellent position for practicing speech. Have the child bite down on the firm object at the molars on one side and then another. Use: tongue depressors, straws of various sizes, toothpicks, coffee stirers, Toothette sticks, swizzle sticks, mouth guard pieces, bite blocks, bitestix, firm rubber tubing, narrow rubber tubing, small chew toys, and so forth.

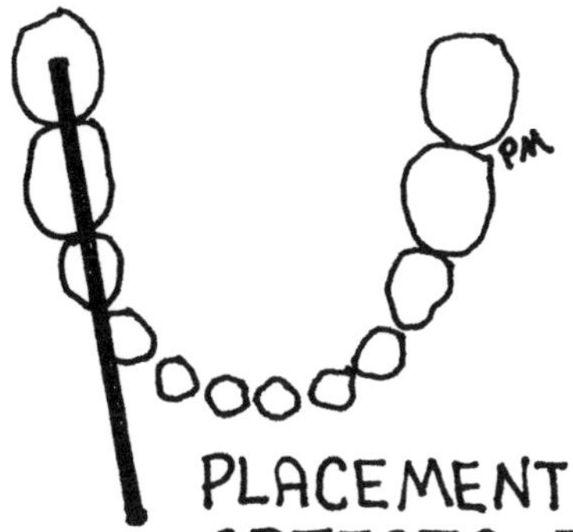

PLACEMENT OF OBJECTS FOR STABILITY

C. Cups: Around two years of age, children naturally begin to stabilize the jaw by biting on a cup when drinking. We can use cup-rim biting with empty plastic cups during vocal play. The cup will stabilize the jaw, and it will provide slight amplification of the produced sounds. Use: drinking cups, stacker cups, or funnels, or use empty individual applesauce, pudding or yogurt cups.

4. Pressure, Tapping and Vibrating

Pressure, tapping and vibration are used to increase awareness of the jaw and its movements. They can be used to increase masseter strength for the bite and chew, and to increase range of jaw movement. Each technique has different effects depending upon how it is used.

A. Apply Pressure to the Masseter: Deep pressure on tight masseters can relax them. Deep pressure on loose masseters will help fire them, especially when the client is asked to bite or chew. Use the finger tip pads to press into each masseter simultaneously.

B. Tap the Masseter: Tapping a loose masseter will tighten it when the client is asked to bite or chew. Use the finger tip pads to tap the masseter.

C. Stretch the Masseter: Place your finger tips on the masseters and massage them up and down carefully in fairly quick stokes in order to increase tone. Ask the client to "Bite here."

D. Vibrate the Masseter: Allow the client to play with a battery or electrically powered vibrator to increase awareness of the jaw and the masseters, and to slightly increase tone by placing the vibrator anywhere on the mandible. Honor the child's reaction to the vibrator, but encourage him to play with it. Use manual vibration by taking hold of the jaw and vibrating it gently and slowly to facilitate increased awareness of the jaw as a separate body part from the head and lower tone. CAUTION! DO NOT INJURE THE TMJ!

Chapter Four Summary

Chapter Four has presented foundational information about the jaw including its movement, problems in its movements and treatment techniques to stabilize and mobilize the jaw.

In the next chapter we shall discuss lip movements in articulation.

Chapter 5

The Lips

Chapter Contents

1. Basic Muscle Review
2. Lip Movements in Speech
3. Lip Movements in Speech Development
4. Diagnosing Lip Movements
5. Problems in Lip Movements
6. Lip Retraction
7. A Hierarchy of Lip Therapy
8. Techniques to Reduce Lip Retraction
9. Tactile and Proprioceptive Stimulation Techniques to Activate the Lips
10. Feeding Therapy Techniques to Activate the Lips
11. Voluntary Lip Exercises to Increase Awareness and Control of Lip Movement

In this chapter we discuss lip movements in speech: (1) how the lips move in mature speech, (2) problems with lip movements seen in the speech-impaired population, and (3) techniques to facilitate improved lip movements.

Basic Muscle Review

In discussing lip movements, it is important to remember that there is only one intrinsic lip muscle — the orbicularis oris. All others which control lip movements are facial muscles. As a result, many of the lip control problems we see in the clinic are actually facial muscle problems. Further, many techniques to inhibit abnormal lip movements and to facilitate more normal lip movements are directed to the face.

For review, the following schematic illustration of the intrinsic and extrinsic lip muscles is offered. Please refer back to it as you read through the text.

Lip Movements in Speech

Lip movements in mature speech are fairly straightforward and easy to observe:

1. The lips meet together for production of the bi-labial phonemes /p/, /b/ and /m/.

2. The lower lip articulates with the upper incisors for production of the labiodental phonemes /f/ and /v/.

3. The lips purse (pucker) for various consonants and vowels.

4. The lips retract (pull back) for various consonants and vowels.

Lip Movements in Speech Development

Lip movement development in speech is interrelated with jaw movement development in speech. When the bi-labials first emerge in early babbling, they are produced with large up-and-down movements of the jaw and little actual lip movement. This pattern is still in use when early words emerge. Over time and as the jaw becomes more stabile, the lips become more active, and mature labial function is seen.

One of the most fascinating aspects of the lips is that they do not have to move at all for production of the labial sounds. When the jaw can move up-and-down, its movements alone can cause the emergence of the labial sounds. For this reason, clients with limited facial expression, limited lip mobility, and even those with facial paralysis can produce the labial sounds.

Diagnosing Lip Movements

To diagnose lip movements, observe the lips: (1) at rest, (2) in spontaneous and imitated speech tasks, (3) in oral-motor imitation tasks and (4) in feeding.

1. Rest Posture: Observe the position and movements of the lips when the child's mouth is at rest — meaning that he is not involved in speech, feeding or oral-motor play behavior. The lips should be resting together gently.

2. Articulation Testing: Note the position and movement of the lips during connected speech and during articulation testing. Note how the lips move during production of bilabials and during production of all other speech sounds.

3. Oral-Motor Exam and Imitation Tasks: Observe lip function during the oral exam and during oral-motor imitation tasks. Also, observe lip positioning during your assessment of tactile stimulation, and note how the lips function before, during and after this stimulation.

4. Feeding: Observe the lips when the child is eating and drinking. Note differences in lip mobility when the child is eating foods of various thickness, textures and wetness. Note the position of the lips during cup-drinking, biting, chewing, food transfer, swallowing and lip cleaning. Also note the position of the lips as the cup or utensil approaches the mouth. Additional training in feeding therapy will aid in this aspect of the assessment.

5. Consultation with Motor Therapists: A complete assessment of lip mobility should be concluded with consultation from motor specialists when a client has a pervasive neuromuscular disorder or fine and gross motor delay. These team members can identify problems in overall tactile sensitivity, tone, reflexes, balance, and hip, shoulder, neck and head position which can help thoroughly assess the causes of the client's lip problems.

Problems in Lip Movements

When clients have difficulty with lip mobility, the cause usually is one of absent or weak movement, and lack of good lip mobility can be traced in most cases to two main problems: lack of tone or excessive tone in the face and lips.

1. Lack of Tone in the Lips

Lack of tone, or hypotonicity, in the lips and face renders the lips slow, weak or completely absent in movement. The lips may appear somewhat large, and the lower lip may appear to sag downward. The lips may be inactive in speech, feeding, in imitation and at rest. Oral rest position may be characterized by open lips rest posture. Hypotonicity in the lips often is associated with oral-tactile hyposensitivity and the reverse swallow pattern. Oral habits, such as thumb sucking, may be contributing to lack of lip movement, as may oral-structural differences such as the anterior open bite.

Treatment for face and lip hypotonicity is directed toward: (a) eliminating contributing oral habits, (b) eliminating contributing oral structural differences, (c) increasing overall oral tone in the face and lips, (d) increasing lip strength, (e) establishing a closed lips rest posture, (f) normalizing oral-tactile sensitivity, (g) facilitating the production of labial consonants, and (h) facilitating the use of lip rounding and lip retracting on vowels and consonants.

2. Excessive Tone in the Lips

Excessive tone, or hypertonicity, in the lips results in lip retraction. When the lip muscles are tight, the lips are drawn away from midline in the direction that the muscles are pulling. Tightness in muscle groups around the mouth cause the lips themselves to be limited in their mobility. Hypertonicity in the face and lips often is associated with oral-tactile hypersensitivity. Tactile hypersensitivity and muscle hypertonicity in the rest of the body may contribute directly to excessive tone in the face and lips.

Treatment for hypertonicity in the face and lips is directed toward: (a) eliminating contributing oral habits, (b) eliminating contributing oral structural differences, (c) decreasing overall oral tone in the face and lips, (d) decreasing lip retraction, (e) establishing a closed lips rest posture, (f) normalizing oral-tactile sensitivity, (g) facilitating appropriate lip mobility, (h) facilitating the production of labial consonants, and (i) facilitating the use of lip rounding and lip retracting on vowels and consonants.

Lip Retraction

Lip retraction is defined as a drawing back of the lips away from midline. It occurs in the following ways:

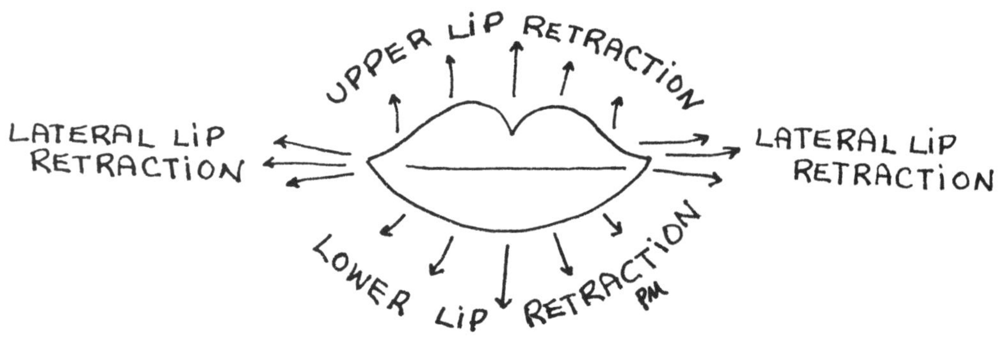

1. Upper Lip Retraction

Upper lip retraction is a pulling upward of the upper lip so that the upper teeth are exposed and the client appears to "sneer." In upper lip retraction, the orbicularis oris itself is not tight. Instead, upper lip retraction is caused by tightening in the upper extrinsic muscles of the lips. Therapy is directed toward reducing or inhibiting the tightness in the muscles above the upper lip and facilitating active upper lip movement.

2. Lower Lip Retraction

Lower lip retraction is a a pulling downward of the lower lip which usually exposes the lower teeth. It should not be confused with hypotonicity in which the lower lip is loose and "hanging." In lower lip retraction, the orbicularis oris itself is not tight. Instead, lower lip retraction is caused by tightening in the lower extrinsic muscles of the lips. Therapy is directed toward reducing or inhibiting the tightness in the muscles below the lower lip and facilitating active lower lip movement.

3. Lateral Lip Retraction

Lateral lip retraction is a pulling laterally of the corners of the mouth so that the client appears to smile. It should not be confused with smiling. In lateral lip retraction, the orbicularis oris itself is not tight. Instead, lateral lip retraction is caused by tightening in the lateral extrinsic muscles of the lips. Therapy is directed toward reducing or inhibiting the tightness in the muscles lateral to the lips and facilitating active upper and lower lip movements.

4. Combinations

All three types described above can occur in any combination.

Slight lip retraction occurs fairly commonly in the articulation-impaired population and is not restricted to clients with obvious neurological impairment. Lip retraction, even in slight amounts, can interfere with bilabial and labiodental sounds although it has not been described in the articulation or phonological therapy literature. Lip retraction is commonly associated with jaw and tongue retraction and can be a tip-off that tongue retraction is present.

Suzanne Evans Morris has described many causes of lip retraction:

1. Head Position: The child who habitually holds his head tipped in a backward direction may find it harder to close the mouth and slight amounts of lip retraction can be

seen. As the head tilts back, a slight pulling of the musculature on either side of the mouth is felt due to the stretch on the lower lip musculature.

2. Shoulders Position: The child with shoulder retraction (shoulder adduction) will usually tip the head back and jut the chin out. Lip retraction commonly results.

3. Hip Position: The child with too much hip extension will experience an overall increase in muscle tone. This increases tone in the face which subsequently increases the possibility that the lips will retract.

4. Tactile Sensitivity: The child who is hypersensitive around the mouth, neck or shoulder girdle often tucks in the chin (retracts the jaw) and retracts the tongue and lips. The response is considered a protective one.

5. General Sensitivity Level: The child who is overly sensitive to any kind of sensory stimulation may retract the lips in an overly stimulating environment.

A Hierarchy of Lip Therapy

Therapy for the lips is organized around a five part "hierarchy of thinking":

1. Reduce or eliminate the effects of lip retraction.
2. Encourage oral-exploratory play.
3. Stimulate lip activity.
4. Strengthen lip movements.
5. Increase voluntary control of lip movements.

Techniques to Reduce Lip Retraction

Techniques to reduce lip retraction can be incorporated into articulation, feeding and motor therapy. When lip retraction is reduced or eliminated during speech therapy activities, children experience more normal movement patterns of the lips. When therapy addresses retraction in the lips, jaw and tongue together, the client experiences more normal movement patterns of the whole mouth. The following techniques are suggested for reducing lip retraction:

1. General Techniques

A. Attend to Positioning: Consult with your team occupational or physical therapist about activities to reduce the effects of poor hip, shoulder, neck and head position when clients have neuromuscular disorder or gross motor and fine motor delay. This should be your first area of consideration since reduction or elimination of these problems often will reduce or eliminate problems with lip retraction. Therapy suggestions might include sitting in a more upright position or working in a flexed position.

B. Attend to Movement: Consult with your team occupational or physical therapist about movement activities which can reduce overall tone. Under the influence of prescribed rotation or gentle rocking to reduce overall body tone, lip retraction can be reduced or eliminated.

C. Reduce Stimuli: Suzanne Evans Morris recommends reducing external distractions for children who demonstrate increased lip retraction in an overly stimulating environment. For example: (1) place the child in individual or small group therapy instead of expecting him to function in a large group, (2) use quiet background music or music with a tempo of 60 beats per minute to create a calm environment in therapy, (3) calm your voice in therapy, (4) watch out for hidden and overt tensions which build in therapy such as competitive games and (5) avoid a visually stimulating environment.

D. Normalize Overall Tactile Sensitivity: Include activities to normalize overall tactile sensitivity before or during articulation, oral-motor and feeding therapy.

2. Oral Techniques

A. Normalize Oral-Tactile Sensitivity: Incorporate games, activities and techniques to normalize oral-tactile hypersensitivity. As oral-tactile sensitivity reduces, increased oral play will emerge and subsequent increases in lip mobility should be seen.

B. Massage the Face: Massage and/or stroke the face slowly and deeply on the muscles which are tight. Begin distally and work medially (toward the lips). Work both sides simultaneously or alternate from one side to the other. Use verbal descriptions such as, "Let go," "Let me have your cheeks" or "Relax here." After the client relaxes the face, slowly release your hold while encouraging him to keep his face "soft," "quiet" or "relaxed."

C. Reduce Upper Lip Retraction: To reduce upper lip retraction: (1) place your fingers on either side of the child's nose and stroke downward toward the bottom of the upper lip, or (2) stroke downward from the center of the cheekbones to the corners of the mouth, or (3) give firm intermittent pressure to the upper lip by pressing it.

REDUCE UPPER LIP RETRACTION

D. Reduce Lateral Lip Retraction: To reduce lateral lip retraction: (1) gently take hold of the cheek by placing your thumb inside the mouth on the inner cheek wall at a point between the upper and lower molars, and your fingers outside the mouth on the cheek, and slowly pull the cheek forward sliding your fingers and thumb towards the corner of the mouth, or (2) place your hands on either cheek and pull slightly forward on the face to make a "fish face" or (3) take the child's face with one hand by placing your thumb on one cheek and your fingers on the other and pull forward gently to make a "fish face."

E. Reduce Lower Lip Retraction: To reduce lower lip retraction, take hold of the chin on either side of midline and massage by pulling it toward midline.

Tactile and Proprioceptive Stimulation Techniques to Activate the Lips

Direct tactile and proprioceptive stimulation can be used to facilitate lip mobility. The following techniques will facilitate lip movement when it is entirely absent, and they will increase awareness and control of lip movement. They can be used with clients who have no ability to understand your directions.

1. Hands-On Pressure: Place your flat finger on the orbicularis oris and maintain firm pressure. When the lips are completely inactive, you may not feel anything right away. After several presentations and over time you should begin to feel muscle activity in the form of twitching under your finger. Encourage the client to move the lips.

2. Hands-Off Pressure: Have the client press his face into a large, round soft object such as a stuffed animal or large soft ball. Make bi-labial sounds against the object.

3. Vibration: Use manual vibration to the orbicularis oris while applying firm and light touch pressure. Encourage the client to move the lips.

4. Stretch: Place both your index finger tips on the orbicularis oris one on either side of midline, and apply stretch pressure to it by stretching from the midline toward both sides simultaneously. To add voluntary control, ask the client to pucker the lips against your resistance.

5. Sucking: Have the client suck on a fairly large round object with the lips. Use: bananas, large teething toys, Popsicles, chunks of ice or adult-size pacifiers.

6. Resistance: Use your finger or another firm object to push upward on the upper lip, and ask the child to pull it down as you push it up. Also push downward on the lower lip, and ask the client to pull it up as you push it down.

7. Stretch: Take hold of the upper lip above the vermillion border by placing the index finger on one side of midline and the thumb on the other. Pinch gently and pull forward. Ask the client to pull the lips away (smile). Most clients will pull the head back instead of using the facial muscles or lips, and you may have to tell them, "Don't use your head. Smile. Use your lips."

8. Stretch: Sit behind the child and place your finger tips on either cheek at the corners of the lips. Draw the face back toward the ears to stretch the lip musculature. Ask the client to pucker the lips against this stretch.

Feeding Therapy Techniques To Activate the Lips

Spoon feeding, cup drinking and straw drinking to stimulate and strengthen lip closure are done during feeding therapy, but they can be incorporated easily into articulation therapy by adding a few snacks to treatment. They are designed to facilitate lip closure when it is entirely absent.

1. Spoon Feeding Technique: Morris recommends using a spoon with a fairly flat bowl, and makes several suggestions. When presenting food, put the spoon straight in and out of the mouth. When inside the mouth, press the bowl of the spoon downward gently but firmly against the tongue. This downward pressure frequently will stimulate the upper lip to draw downward. In any case, wait a few seconds while the spoon is inside for the upper lip to descent. Then draw the spoon out.

2. Cup Drinking: As in spoon feeding, cup drinking activities can be used in feeding therapy or as part of oral-motor activities in articulation therapy. A cup, glass, small bowl or cut-out cup can be used. Thick liquids are used such as: strained fruit, pudding or custard which is thinned with water to the desired consistency. Also use: fruit nectar or a combination of custard and milk, or ice cream and milk. With the head in correct alignment, and with oral control used as needed, present the liquid slowly so that it touches the upper lip. If tactile responses have been normalized correctly, the stimulus of the liquid, especially if the liquid is cold, will facilitate downward movement of the upper lip.

3. Straw Drinking: Straw drinking usually is introduced only after the child can swallow liquids from a cup. It can be an effective tool in the stimulation of lip closure if a few adaptations are made. Place the straw on the lower lip in front of the teeth. Experiment with straws and flexible vinyl tubing of various diameters. Place a small round plastic disk with a hole drilled in the center on the end of the straw to regulate the amount of straw that goes into the mouth and to provide tactile stimulation to the lips. Or, wind a rubberband around the end of the straw to increase the size and texture of the straw end. Make sure it can not be sucked off and swallowed! Suck liquids of various consistencies from thick to thin.

Voluntary Lip Exercises to Increase Awareness and Voluntary Control of Lip Movement

Lip exercises require a considerable amount of voluntary movement control on the part of the client. They can be used in oral exploratory play or in structured activities. They include:

1. Smiling: Smile into an exaggerated /i/ position (retract the lips) and hold it.

2. Puckering: Pucker the lips and hold it.

3. Pursing: Purse the lips and hold it.

4. Resisting: Close the lips against resistance.

5. Pressing: Close the lips on a tongue depressor while the therapist tries to pull it out.

6. Pressing: Maintain lip closure while the therapist tries to pry the lips open.

7. Broad Smiling: Smile broadly alternating with the lips closed and with the lips open.

8. Frowning: Frown tightly and hold it.

9. Alternate Movements: Alternate lip pursing and retracting.

10. Produce Labial Phonemes: Practice phonemes, syllables and words with /u,m,b,p,w/.

11. Puff the Cheeks: Puff up up the cheeks with the lips tightly closed to prevent air leak.

12. Blow Toward Objects: Blow cotton balls, pinwheels and bubbles.

13. Blow Into Objects: Blow into horns, whistles, kazoos, harmonicas, etc.

14. Produce Raspberries: "Play" with bi-labial and lingua-labial voiced and voiceless raspberries.

15. Pull On a Button: Tie a piece of dental floss to a large button. Place the button flat between the lips and front teeth. Tug gently on the floss and encourage the child to hold the button in place with his lips.

16. Use Lip Retractors: Lip retractors pull the lips laterally to expose all the teeth. (They are used by dental practitioners for x-raying and photographing.) Ask the client to try to approximate the lips while the retractor is in place.

17. Use a Lip Exerciser: Lip exercisers are now available commercially. Place between lips and alternate contraction and retraction.

18. Practice Spaghetti Pulls: Place one end of a piece of cooked spaghetti noodle between the teeth, and use the lips to draw the rest in.

19. Lip Massage: Place the lower lip on the upper one and massage downward.

20. Lip Gym: Place a lip gym between the lips and teeth. Tug gently and ask the client to press the lips in and hold the gym in place.

Chapter Five Summary

Chapter Five has presented information about the lips and their movements for speech. We have discussed how the lips should move in speech, problems occur in the speech population, techniques to inhibit inappropriate lip movements, and techniques to facilitate improved lip mobility and their voluntary control.

Chapter 6

The Tongue

Chapter Contents

1. Historic Divisions of the Tongue
2. Palatography
3. Differential Tongue Movement Patterns in Speech
4. Functional Zones of the Tongue
5. Stability and Mobility in Tongue Movement
6. Summary of Tongue Movements in Speech
7. A New Concept of Tongue Movement
8. Tongue Movements in Swallowing
9. The "Normal" Tongue Configuration
10. Tongue Movement Problems
11. Facilitating Basic Tongue Movement Patterns

This chapter is about the tongue: (1) its movements, (2) the development of its movements, (3) the diagnosis of its movements, and (4) techniques for remediation of the tongue's movement problems in speech delay and disorder. The entire chapter is based on a new concept of tongue mobility.

Historic Divisions of the Tongue

Historically the tongue has been described as being comprised of four basic sections from front to back — tip, blade, body and back — and two sections left and right of midline.

This linear view of the tongue and its movements has been the cornerstone of phonetics and articulation therapy for many years. Although this model of the tongue is interesting and has historic value, its presentation poorly represents how the tongue actually moves during speech and feeding tasks.

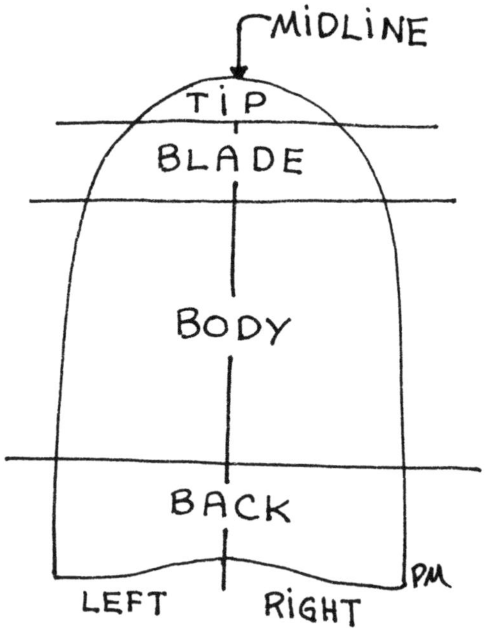

HISTORIC DIVISIONS OF THE TONGUE

A careful analysis of that which we know about tongue movements from palatography, dysphagia and infant developmental feeding research, along with a fresh careful look at articulation itself, teaches us that the tongue moves in patterns which are more curved, more graceful and ultimately more powerful than the historic perspective leads one to believe. Mature tongue movements are the ultimate result of complete differentiation of the tongue from the jaw.

Palatography

The tongue and its movements can be understood quite well by considering its areas of articulation with the palate, information gained through the study of palatography. Palatography provides an aerial view of tongue movements in speech, which allows us to map where the tongue touches the palate during the production of single phonemes. The resultant maps — or palatograms — allow us to see the tongue's articulation with the palate in two dimensions: from front-to-back and from side-to-side.

Two basic procedures for acquiring palatograms have been developed:

1. Historical Palatography

In historical palatography procedures, an atomizer (a dust sprayer) is used to dust the hard palate, the lingual surfaces of the teeth, and the soft palate with a dark powder made of one part charcoal dust to two parts chocolate powder. A subject is asked to utter a target sound and then open the mouth. A photograph is taken of the roof of the mouth as it reflects in a mirror. The photograph reveals that the dust is removed where the tongue has made contact and remains where it has not. The photograph becomes a permanent record of the tongue's articulation with the palate during production of that sound.

2. Electropalatography

In more recent times, electropalatography has been used for this same purpose. A false palate is made for a single subject and embedded with electrodes. These are wired to a computer which displays in real time the areas of contact between the tongue and the palate.

Palatography, whether done the old fashioned way or with computer technology, has given us good information about the position of the tongue as it contacts the roof of the mouth — it gives us a good two-dimensional aerial view. Results of these studies are presented schematically and interpreted below.

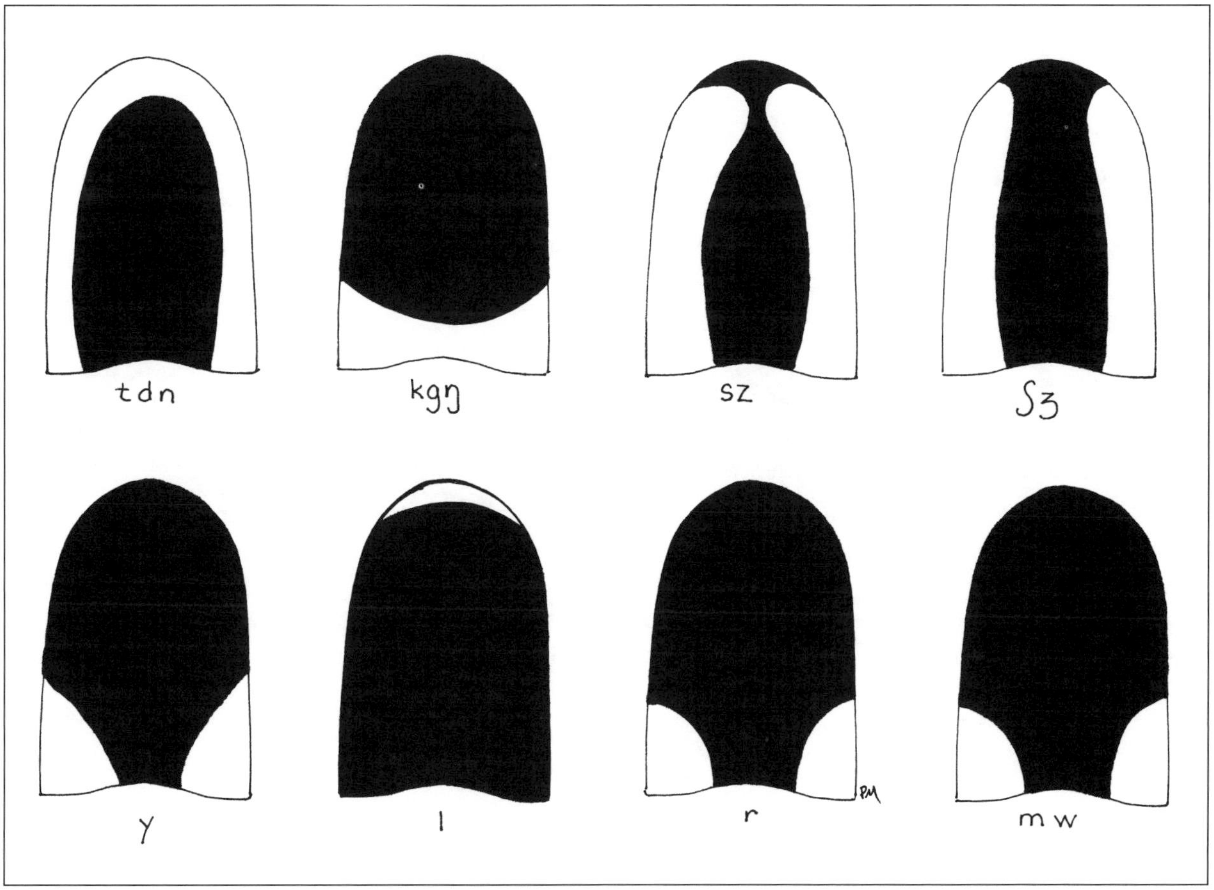

The Palatograms

It is important to keep in mind that these are schematic illustrations of palates and not tongues. The light part of each palatogram is the place where the tongue has made contact with the palate, and the dark part is where it has not. Study each palatogram above carefully as you read the following interpretations. The palatograms shed tremendous light on how the tongue actually moves during speech.

Differential Tongue Movement Patterns in Speech

The palatograms teach us how the tongue positions itself for speech sound productions, and from these we can understand how the tongue moves for speech. The basic tongue movement patterns are described:

1. Horseshoe-Shape Elevation

The first basic pattern is the horseshoe-shape which can be seen in the production of phonemes /t/, /d/ and /n/. These phonemes are made with the tongue touching the palate in a horseshoe-shape around the perimeter while the middle section of the tongue stays down and away from the palate. The pattern is used to occlude airflow through the oral cavity — allowing airflow to be stopped for production of the stops and for it to be directed out the nose for the nasal /n/. Essentially, the tongue on-glides into the horseshoe-shape position, and then off-glides by lowering the tip while the sides remain high.

This view contradicts the traditional view that has categorized these sounds as lingua-alveolar which suggested that these phonemes are made with lingua-alveolar contact alone. Lingua-alveolar contact alone would prohibit the production of these sounds because the tongue would be unable to "stop" airflow or to direct it nasally. The horseshoe-shape of tongue contact to the palate ensures that the oral flow of air is occluded or is redirected to the nose.

• Oral Movement Lessons: We learn two things about tongue movement from these palatograms of /t/, /d/ and /n/: (1) the tongue is able to lift its sides and tip up toward the palate in a simultaneous horseshoe-shape gesture while (2) keeping the middle section down. The horseshoe-shape is a foundational concept of tongue mobility.

• Additional Phonemes Which Use This Pattern: Variations of the basic horseshoe-shape movement patterns are seen on voiced and voiceless "th." These cognates are also produced with horseshoe-shape articulation, but in this case, the articulation courses from the palate to the teeth.

2. Back Elevation

The second basic tongue movement pattern noted on the palatograms is independent elevation of the tongue back. This can be seen in the production of phonemes /k/, /g/ and /ng/. Phonemes /k/, /g/ and "ng" are made with the tongue touching the palate across the back while the forward section of the tongue stays down and away from the palate. This view supports the traditional view that these phonemes are made with lingua-velar contact alone.

• Oral Movement Lessons: From these palatograms we learn: (1) the tongue is able to lift its back third while (2) keeping the anterior two-thirds down and away from the palate. Elevation of the tongue's entire back is a foundational concept of tongue mobility.

• Additional Phonemes Which Use This Pattern: Variations on tongue back elevation are seen in the form of how much of the back is used. Notice that almost all phonemes are made with part or all of the back of the tongue articulating with the palate during their production.

3. Lateral Elevation

The third basic tongue movement pattern is elevation of the sides which can be seen in the production of the sibilants. Sibilant phonemes are made with the tongue touching the palate along the sides while the tip and middle sections stay down and away from the palate in a groove. Even if the tongue-tip elevates for the sibilants as it does for some people, it elevates without touching the palate.

The most important feature of sibilant production is that the sides of the tongue articulate with the palate while the middle of the tongue stays down along the tongue's length. If the sides do not articulate along their length, air leakage will result laterally causing a lateral lisp. If a midline groove cannot be accomplished, midline air stream cannot be formed and a frontal or lateral lisp results.

• Oral Movement Lessons: The palatograms for the sibilants teach us that: (1) the tongue can elevate simultaneously along its sides while (2) the middle section stays down through the tongue's length. Articulating the sides while allowing air to flow medially over the middle sections of the tongue is the foundation movement pattern of all sibilants, and each sibilant is produced with a variation on this theme.

• Additional Phonemes Which Use This Pattern: Variations in this tongue movement pattern result from increasing or decreasing the length and width of articulation along the sides, and the width of the midline groove. Notice how production of most consonant phonemes and all the vowels are made with articulation along the sides with the midline groove. Even those phonemes made with the horseshoe-shape on-glide utilize lateral elevation, and that lateral elevation is part of the horseshoe-shape position.

4. Differential Tip Elevation and Depression

The fourth basic tongue movement pattern to be discussed is independent elevation and depression of the tongue tip. Independent tip elevation can be seen in the production of phoneme /l/. For production of /l/, we elevate the tip to the alveolar ridge, and we keep the rest of the tongue low and away from the palate.

• Oral Movement Lessons: From the palatograms involving the tip we learn that: (1) the tip can elevate independently while (2) the entire rest of the tongue can stay down and away from the palate, and (3) the tip can lower independently from the horseshoe-shape while (4) the sides can remain high.

• Additional Phonemes Which Use This Pattern: Independent depression of the tip can be perceived in production of lingua-alveolar phonemes /t/, /d/, and /n/. After the tongue on-glides into the horseshoe-shape for production of these sounds, it off-glides by lowering the tip.

5. Blade Elevation

Blade elevation usually is not discussed when describing "normal" articulation. Typically, we think of "blading" as an abnormal pattern associated with frontal lisping and interdental tongue placement. However, differential elevation of the blade is necessary for the production of certain sounds, namely phonemes /s/ and /z/.

The palatograms reveal that phonemes /s/ and /z/ are made with elevation of the sides of the tongue from the back forward, and elevation of the blade from the sides toward midline but not touching at midline. Such a position allows for a narrow groove to be formed for air to escape medially. This narrow groove at the blade creates a deep and narrow channel through which air is directed. Its narrowness assures that the air stream will be tight (not diffuse) and the resultant sound will be sharp.

Differential elevation of the blade is a movement pattern which reflects an advanced refinement of tongue movement patterns. This is fine motor tongue control. This view of /s/ and /z/ clearly makes our historical "lingua-alveolar" view of these phonemes seem incorrect. The sides of the tongue need to articulate with the palate all the way along the side teeth in order to prevent air leakage laterally. Simultaneously, the tongue must form a groove down the middle and through the portion of the blade section that elevates to the palate.

• Oral Movement Lesson: From the palatograms for /s/ and /z/ we learn that (1) the tongue can lift its blade section high on the sides while (2) the middle of the blade and the tip can stay down. This is highly refined tongue movement control seen only in mature speech. When this oral movement pattern has not evolved, the client must resort to another movement pattern for production of /s/ and /z/, typically, the frontal lisp.

Functional Zones of the Tongue

Although the tongue is considered one single body part, one can see clearly how it has the ability to move its parts differentially. By superimposing each palatogram one on top of another, we arrive at the conclusion that these are 16 individually moving parts of the tongue which I call the “functional zones” of tongue movement.

The zones have been numbered from one through sixteen for ease in discussion. From this analysis, a new assignment of names for the parts of the tongue are offered:

1. Tip: Zones 1 and 2.
2. Blade: Zones 4, 5, 6 and 7.
3. Lateral Blades: Zones 4 and 7.
4. Middle Blade: Zones 5 and 6.
5. Body: Zones 10-11.
6. Back: Zones 13, 14, 15 and 16.
7. Lateral Backs: Zones 13 and 16.
8. Middle Back: Zones 14 and 15.
9. Left Lateral Margin: Zones 3, 9 and 13.
10. Right Lateral Margin: Zones 8, 12 and 16.

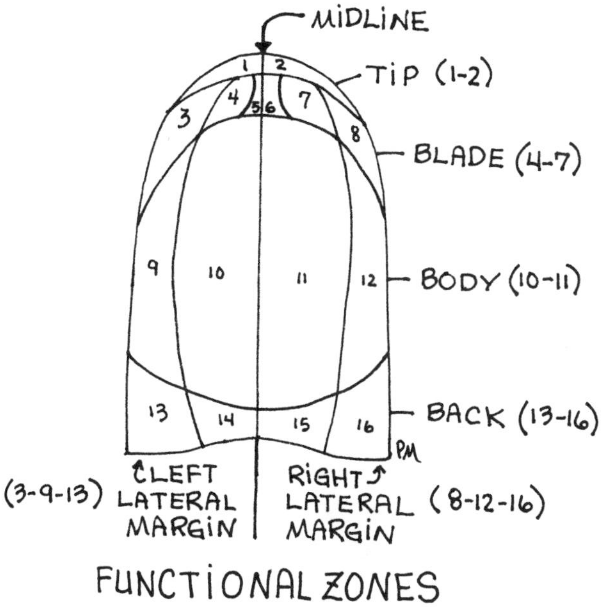

The ability to move each individual part makes for refined and mature articulation of the lingua phonemes. Without the ability to move each part differentially from the rest, phoneme productions must be changed either by substitution, omission or distortion.

Stability and Mobility in Tongue Movement

Our analysis of tongue movements goes deeper when we consider the impact of stability and mobility on the tongue's movements. Principle #4 in The Organization of Motor Control (Chapter Two), states that “all movement is accomplished through an interplay of mobility and stability.” That means that all movements of the tongue are accomplished through a balance of stationary parts and moving parts.

The back-lateral margins of the tongue (zones 13 and 16) are its points of stability.

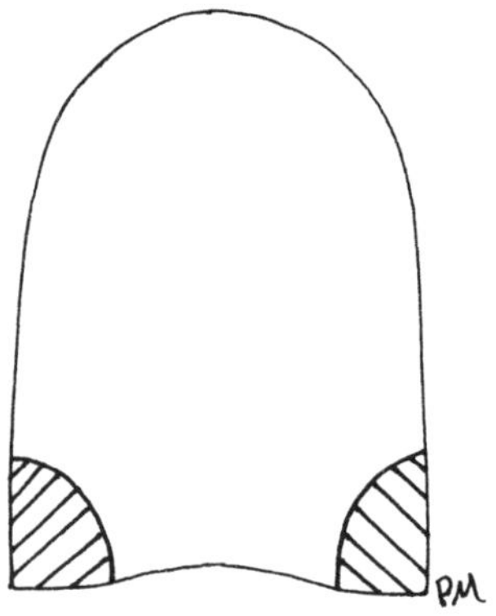

STABILIZING ZONES

Try this experiment with the lingua phonemes: Think about the back-lateral margins (zones 13 and 16) of your tongue as you produce the lingua phonemes. Take a moment to bite gently on these back sides, and to rub these sections of the tongue back-and-forth against the lower surfaces of your upper molars. This is to heighten sensation there. Now, think about these zones 13 and 16 as you say all the lingua sounds in syllables. Say:

Dee-dee-dee	
Tee-tee-tee	Shee-shee-shee
Nee-nee-nee	Zhee-zhee-zhee
See-see-see	Chee-chee-chee
Zee-zee-zee	Jee-jee-jee
	Kee-kee-kee
	Gee-gee-gee

Notice that as you produce each sequence, the tongue's lateral back sections never leave their position near the palate. Even when we produce back sounds /k/ and /g/, the lateral backs remain stationary while the middle back elevates and depresses.

Try another experiment with the bi-labials: Now, say "bee-bee-bee-bee-bee," "me-me-me-me-me," and "we-we-we-we-we" in the same way. As you produce these bi-labial sequences, do you feel the back lateral margins of the tongue stabilizing while the rest of the mouth moves? Look at the palatograms for /m/, /b/ and /w/. Notice how the tongue's back-lateral margins articulate with the palate during production of these sounds even though we consider them labial sounds.

Try another experiment with the alphabet: Now, think about these two parts (Zones 13 and 16) as you recite the alphabet aloud in a rapid conversational speech style. Notice what these parts of the tongue do as you speak.

"ABCDEFGHIJKLMNOPQRSTUVWXYZ"

Did you notice that the back-lateral margins stay relatively put while the rest of the tongue moves up-and-down, all around them? The only exception may be when you say "L."

Try one more experiment with connected speech: Read this paragraph aloud and put your attention on the tongue's back lateral margins. Do you notice that the these two sections stay up next to the palate or upper molars the whole time? Again, the only exception should be when you say /l/.

The back lateral margins of the tongue can be viewed as the "shoulders" of the tongue. Just like the the arms and legs are outgrowths of the body, so too are the head and tongue. Just as the shoulders are the points of stability for the arms, so too are the back lateral margins the points of stability for the tongue.

The back lateral margins of the tongue appear to be the points of stability for ALL speech movements, not just tongue movements. We maintain back-lateral tongue stability throughout all speech.

This being the general rule, of course, there must be exceptions to it. When we speak in a loud voice or a voice conducive to public speaking and singing, we open the mouth further than we do for conversational speech. As a result, we pull the tongue completely away from the palate. Even so, the tongue continues to move from this relatively fixed and stable position. Internal stability — the ability of a body part to maintain stability inherently — takes over and assures that the tongue's neutral position will be honored throughout the speech event.

Summary of Tongue Movements in Speech

The palatograms and the concept of stability and mobility have taught us that the tongue moves in well-defined differential movement patterns for speech. A description of these and the names which can be assigned to the movements follow:

1. The sides and tip of the tongue can elevate together as a unit differentially from the rest of the tongue (HORSESHOE-SHAPE ELEVATION).

2. The sides of the tongue can elevate simultaneously and differentially from the tip and the rest of the tongue (LATERAL MARGIN ELEVATION).

3. The tip of the tongue can elevate and depress differentially from the sides and the rest of the tongue (TIP ELEVATION AND DEPRESSION).

4. The back of the tongue can elevate as a mass differentially from the rest of the tongue (BACK ELEVATION).

5. The middle back can elevate and depress differentially from the lateral back sections (MIDDLE BACK ELEVATION AND DEPRESSION).

6. The blade of the tongue can elevate differentially from the tip (BLADE ELEVATION).

7. The two lateral blade sections can elevate simultaneously and differentially from the middle blade (LATERAL BLADE ELEVATION).

8. The middle of the tongue never articulates with the palate during mature speech (MIDDLE DEPRESSION).

A New Concept of Tongue Movement

A new concept of tongue movement in speech arises from our analysis. The tongue moves for speech by: (1) stabilizing at the back lateral margins, while (2) raising and lowering differential parts of the rest of the perimeter of the tongue, and (3) all the while keeping the middle section down.

The three fundamental movement patterns of the tongue, therefore, are (1) stability, (2) elevation, and (3) depression.

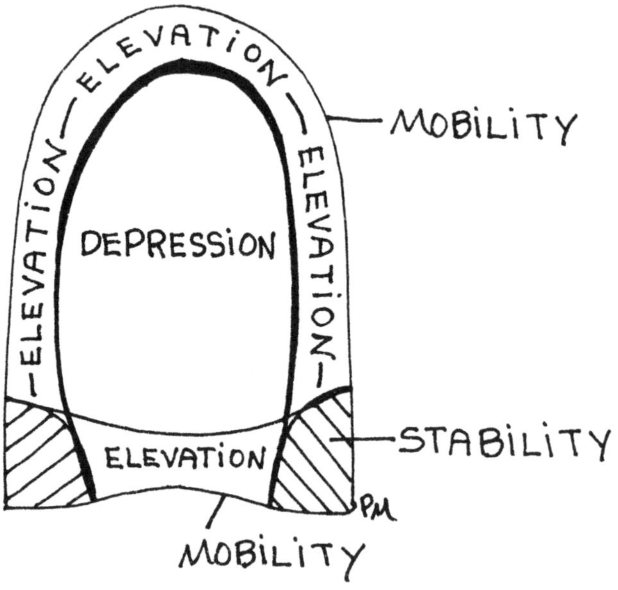

Tongue Movements in Swallowing

Our understanding of tongue mobility would not be complete without data from swallowing research. Studies of the tongue and its movements in swallowing support our new concept of tongue mobility. The process of swallowing has been described in the dysphagia literature as having four stages or phases: the oral preparatory stage, the oral stage, the oral-pharyngeal stage and the esophageal stage. The first two stages are of interest to us since they describe the ways in which the tongue itself moves during the swallow.

1. The Oral Preparatory Stage

The first stage of the swallow has been termed the "Oral Preparatory Stage" since it occurs just before the initiation of the actual swallow — it is movement done in preparation for the swallow. This phase consists of mastication, mixing the food with saliva, gathering the food into a bolus, and holding the bolus in preparation for the actual swallow. In mature eating: (1) the lips are held closed, (2) the jaw moves in a rotary fashion, (3) the cheeks press in towards the molars so that food does not slip in and get caught in the sulci (the space between the cheek and molars), and (4) the tongue moves in many sophisticated ways.

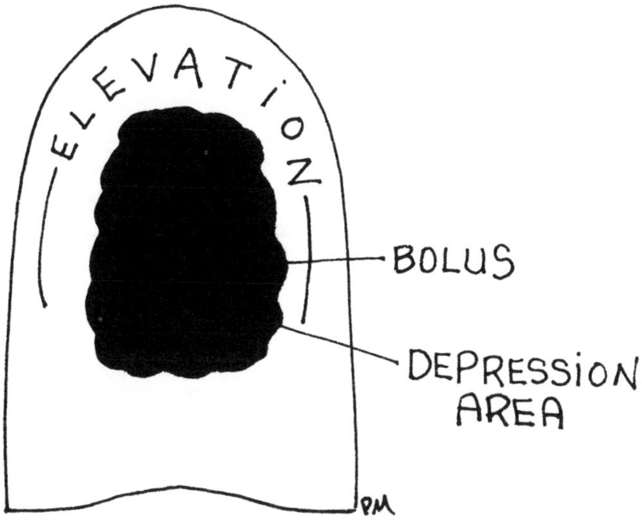

ORAL PREPARATION STAGE

The tongue: (1) is able to take food into the mouth and transfer it from side-to-side, (2) is able to use its lateral margins to hold food at the molars for chewing, (3) is able to sweep the oral cavity clean of food and (4) is able to draw the food into a bolus for swallowing.

Throughout this process, the predominant tongue movement pattern is one of elevating the tongue-tip and lateral margins while the midline remains depressed. In order for food to be drawn into the cohesive bolus for swallowing, the lateral margins and the tip of the tongue must elevate simultaneously and press upwards against the palate while the middle section remains down. This action renders the tongue into a "bowl" or "cup" shape configuration. When the tongue holds the bolus in this horseshoe-shape configuration with tip and lateral margin elevation and midline depression, the end of this first phase is marked.

2. The Oral Stage

The second phase of the swallow has been termed the "Oral Stage" since it describes the movement of the bolus through the oral cavity on its way back to the pharynx. During this phase: (1) the lips continue to remain closed so that food does not leak out (note: if the tongue is used correctly, lip closure is not necessary to prevent leakage in the normal swallow), (2) the jaw is elevated so that bi-labial and tongue-to-palate contact can be made easily, (3) the cheeks do not have to be active since no food should be left in the sulci, and (4) the tongue does the work of propelling the food bolus back into the oropharynx.

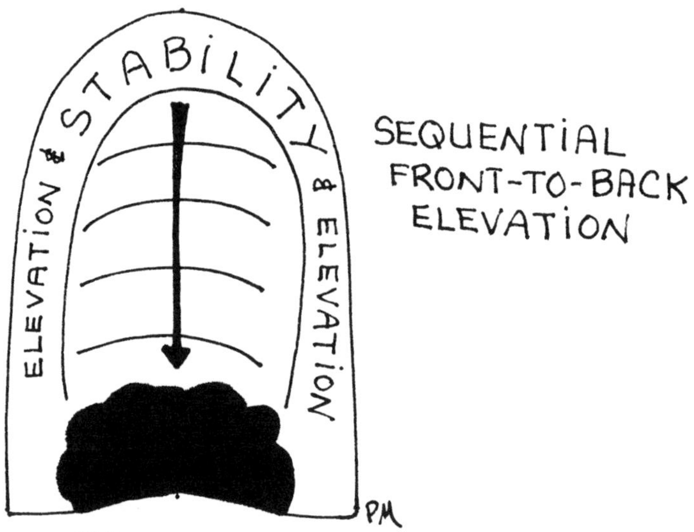

ORAL STAGE

In order to propel the bolus posteriorly: (1) the tongue-tip and lateral margins must remain elevated and sealed against the palate in a horseshoe shape so that no food will escape forward or out the sides, and (2) the middle sections of the tongue elevate towards the palate in a front-to-back stripping action. This action pushes the food back to the back of the tongue where the swallow reflex will be triggered. The triggering of the swallow reflex signals the beginning of the third phase of the swallow.

Both the oral preparatory and the oral stages of the swallow support the concepts we have learned about tongue movements from speech.

The "Normal" Tongue Configuration

When the tongue is "exercised" for years with a correct swallow pattern and correct speech, it takes on a certain "look" or configuration. The tongue, being composed of muscles, responds to exercise just like all muscles in the body do — they become more defined. With proper exercise in speech and feeding, the tongue takes on the characteristic shape represented schematically below.

Upon visual inspection, the tongue should: (1) be flat to concave, (2) extend laterally from the middle through the lateral margins, (3) extend through the tip, and (4) elevate slightly in the tip and lateral margins.

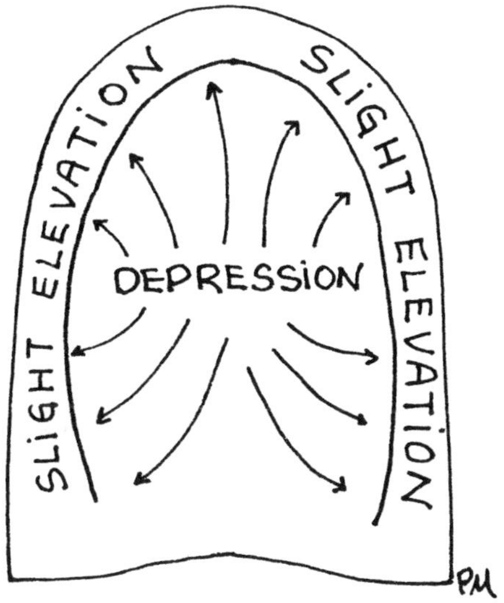

"NORMAL" TONGUE CONFIGURATION

Tongue Movement Problems

When oral-motor development is delayed, disordered or incomplete and the tongue's movement patterns are immature, the movements take on certain patterns which reflect our principles of movement development:

1. Gross-to-Fine

When oral-motor skills are delayed, refined tongue movements are slow to develop and gross tongue movement patterns predominate. As a result, less differential movement in the sixteen functional zones of the tongue is seen. The bigger movement patterns are relied upon and the refined movement patterns are absent.

• Remediation: Therapy needs to be directed toward: (1) facilitating a flat and flared tongue, (2) facilitating lateral extension and elevation, (3) facilitating tip extension and elevation, (4) facilitating back elevation, (5) facilitating middle depression, and (6) facilitating differential blade use.

2. Proximal-to-Distal

When oral-motor control is delayed, the tongue's movements usually are incomplete in their development from proximal-to-distal. As a result, the tongue-tip, which is the most distal or anterior portion of the tongue, appears weak and less well developed. This is noted typically in a tongue-tip which is retracted and a blade that is protruding. The tongue appears thick and blunt through the blade and tip. [Note: This oral-motor delay pattern should not be confused with the restricting lingual frenum which is a structural difference that renders a blunt tip and which pulls the tip inward or downward.]

• Remediation: Therapy needs to be directed toward: (1) maturing overall movement of the tongue, and (2) facilitating tongue-tip extension and elevation.

3. Medial-to-Lateral

When oral-motor control is delayed, the tongue usually is incomplete in its development from medial-to-lateral. This is noted typically in the lateral margins which are retracted toward midline and a middle section that is protruding, rendering the tongue thick in the body and lax on the sides.

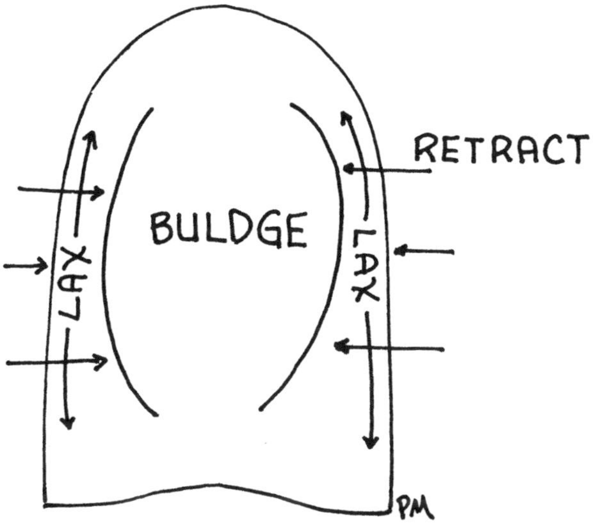

• Remediation: Therapy needs to be directed toward: (1) maturing overall movement of the tongue, (2) facilitating lateral extension and elevation, and (3) depressing the middle section.

4. Hypotonicity

When muscle tone is low: (1) the tongue appears soft, large and bulbous, (2) the tongue may protrude, (3) hyposensitivity often is present, (4) the tip is weak, (5) the lateral margins are weak, (6) less than sixteen functional zones are active, (7) more gross movements are noted, and (8) the tongue may be lax and inactive.

• Remediation: Therapy needs to be directed toward: (1) increasing tone, (2) normalizing oral-tactile sensitivity, (3) facilitating tip extension and elevation, (4) facilitating back elevation, (5) facilitating middle depression, and (6) facilitating differential control.

5. Hypertonicity

When muscle tone is high: (1) the tongue appears hard and narrow but thick in the middle, (2) the tongue may retract, (3) hypersensitivity often is present, (4) the tip typically is retracted into the body of the tongue, (5) the lateral margins typically are retracted medially, (6) less than sixteen functional zones are active, (7) more gross and stiff movements are noted, and (8) the tongue may be inactive.

• Remediation: Therapy needs to be directed toward: (1) decreasing tone, (2) normalizing oral-tactile sensitivity, (3) facilitating tip extension and elevation, (4) facilitating back elevation, (5) facilitating middle depression, (6) facilitating lateral extension and elevation, (7) facilitating differential control, and (8) facilitating rotary movements.

6. Oral-Tactile Sensitivity Problems

Oral-tactile sensitivity problems have a direct effect on tongue movements. Both tactile hypersensitivity and hyposensitivity tend to cause the tongue to move more grossly and with less differentiation.

• Remediation: Therapy needs to be directed toward normalizing oral-tactile sensitivity.

7. Structural Problems

Structural problems have a direct effect on tongue movements, typically causing the tongue to find and settle on unusual movement patterns.

• Remediation: In the ideal setting, therapy needs to be directed toward (1) eliminating the oral structural problem, and (2) teaching appropriate movement patterns. In the less-than-ideal setting, compensatory oral movements need to be taught.

8. Oral Habit Problems

Oral habits (such as long term thumb sucking) can have a direct effect on tongue movements depending upon their frequency, duration and intensity. Oral habits typically cause the tongue: (1) to have an unusual rest posture, (2) to use a different swallowing pattern, (3) to be delayed in its movement development, and (4) to develop unusual movement patterns.

• Remediation: In the ideal setting, therapy is directed toward: (1) eliminating the oral habit, (2) teaching appropriate oral rest, (3) teaching appropriate swallow, and (4) facilitating appropriate oral movement patterns for speech. When the oral habit can not or will not be eliminated, deviations in tongue position and movement can be expected to remain.

Facilitating Basic Tongue Movement Patterns

Tongue movements can be facilitated through both tactile and proprioceptive stimulation in either hands-on or hands-off procedures. Techniques are designed to facilitate elevation, depression, stability and differentiation in oral exploratory play, feeding or direct learning activities.

Please remember, these techniques are designed to facilitate tongue movement when feeding skill is relatively intact. These techniques will not be enough in the absence of sucking or swallowing skill in clients with severe feeding problems. They are designed to facilitate the emergence of appropriate speech movements.

If you are referring to these techniques before reading the sections above on how the tongue really moves in speech, go back and read! These techniques assume that the jaw is active, mobile and is beginning to stabilize. In the absence of jaw mobility and maturing stability, incorporate the following techniques with those to mobilize and stabilize the jaw.

1. Stimulating the Horseshoe-Shape

The basic horseshoe-shape configuration can be facilitated by stimulating the Tongue-Bowl Response (TBR).

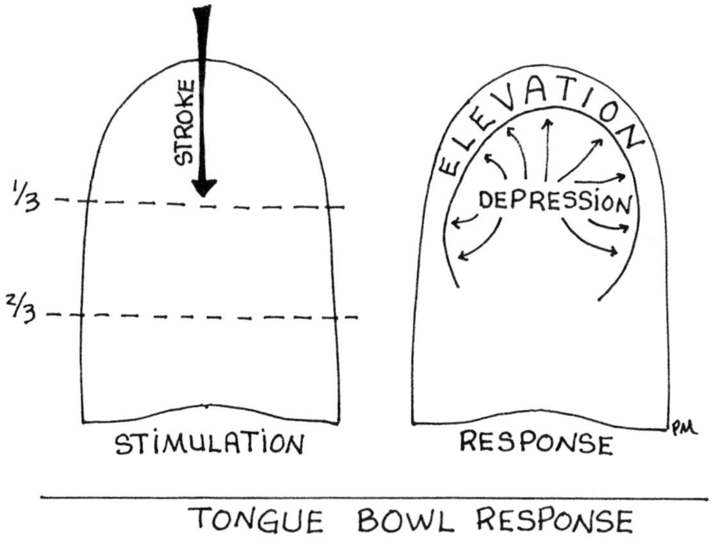

• Stimulation: Tactile stimulation to the anterior 1/3 of the tongue. Use a textured object such as: toothette, infadent toothbrush, toothbrush, or ora-swab.

• Response: The tongue flattens, flairs and forms a bowl shape with tip and lateral margin elevation and midline depression.

The Tongue Bowl Response also has been called the cup-shape configuration, the tongue groove, and the tongue's grasping response. It functions in feeding to accept and pull liquid and food into the oral cavity.

The TBR also can be stimulated in any way which stimulates the middle of the tongue including: (1) filling the mouth with a large object such as a large chew toy once oral-tactile responses are "normal", (2) sucking thick liquids through a straw, (3) pressing a spoon bowl down into the middle of the tongue during spoon feeding, and (4) tapping the middle of the tongue.

2. Stimulating Back Elevation

Back elevation can be facilitated by stimulating the Tongue Retraction Response (TRR).

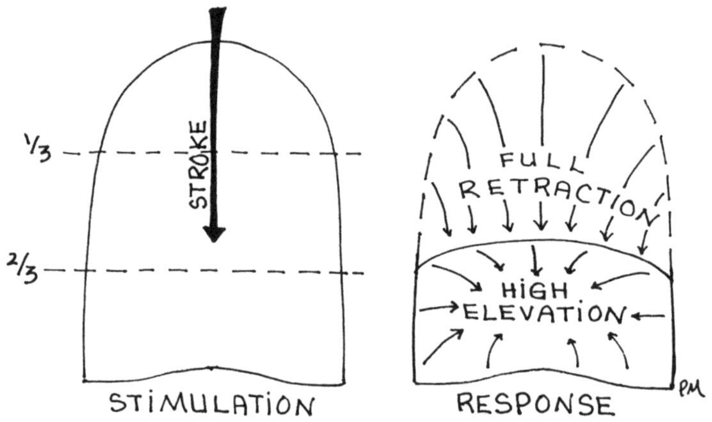

TONGUE RETRACTION RESPONSE

• Stimulation: Stroke down the middle of the tongue to about half-way toward the back. Use a textured object such as: finger, toothbrush, pretzel or other food, mouthing toy, Toothette, Nuk massage brush or Infa-Dent toothbrush.

• Response: The whole tongue humps up and back into a ball-shape which completely fills the posterior oral cavity and occludes the airway.

The Tongue Retraction Response also has been termed the "pre-gag" movement since it occurs before the gag is set off. The TRR prevents foreign objects from going too far back into the oropharynx and prevents the true gag from occurring.

The TRR also can be stimulated by: (1) filling the mouth with a large object such as a large chew toy, or (2) applying deep pressure to the back of the tongue. Deep pressure to the posterior tongue is a "drastic" measure that should be saved for times when nothing else has worked. To accomplish this: (1) place your finger tip on the back of the tongue at midline, (2) press that portion of the tongue downward toward the larynx, (3) press gently but somewhat firmly — be careful! and (4) ask the child to "push up" against your finger.

3. Stimulating Lateral Elevation

Lateral elevation can be facilitated by stimulating the Tongue Lateralization Response (TLR).

•Stimulation: Stroke the sides of the tongue back-and-forth on one side of the tongue and then the other. Use: finger, toothbrush, pretzel or other food, mouthing toy, Toothette, Nuk Massage Brush, Infa-Dent Toothbrush, etc.

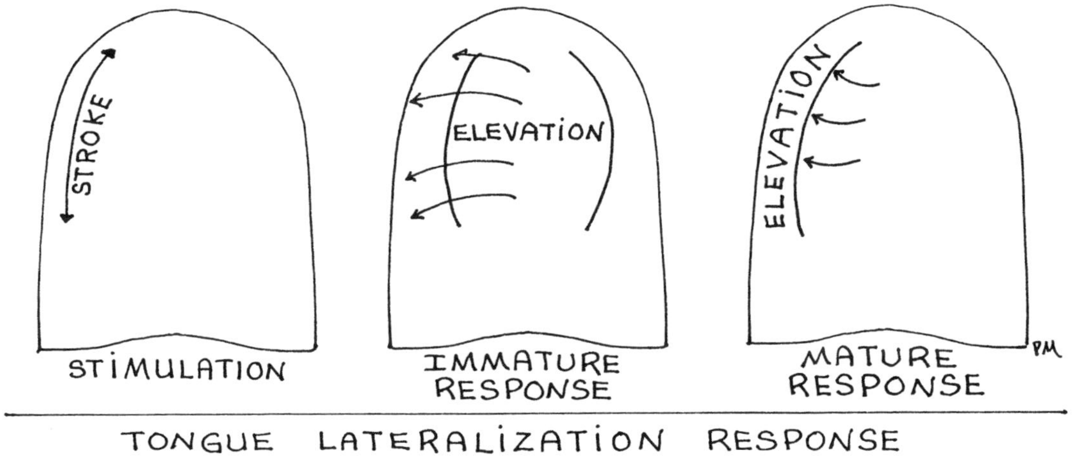

• Immature Response: The whole tongue humps up along midline and rocks to the side of stimulation (this has been terms a "gross rolling action").

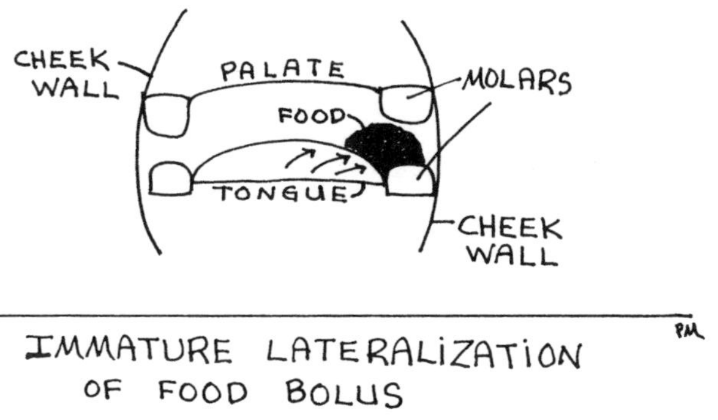

• Mature Response: The lateral margin of the tongue elevates and moves toward the side of stimulation.

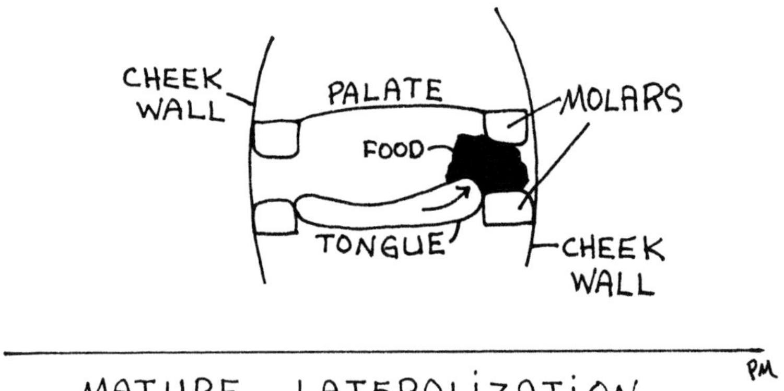

MATURE LATERALIZATION OF FOOD BOLUS

The lateral margins also can be stimulated to elevate independently from the rest of the tongue in other ways:

A. Stimulate the Tongue Bowl Response: This stimulation (see #1 above) will strengthen elevation of the lateral margins.

B. Press Medially: Place a firm object (finger, pretzel, Toothette, tongue depressor, etc.) on the side of the tongue against one length. Push gently but firmly into the side of the tongue toward midline. Ask the client to push laterally against the object.

C. Press Downward on the Top of the Lateral Margins: Place a firm object (finger, pretzel, Toothette, tongue depressor, etc.) on the top of one side of the tongue on the lateral margin. Push down gently but firmly, and ask the client to push upward with that part of the tongue.

D. Stimulate the Palate: Stroke that part of the palate toward which you want the lateral portion of the tongue to move. Say, "Put your tongue up here."

E. Teach Correct Food Transfer: Teach the client to use first the immature and then the mature lateral movements of the tongue to transfer small pieces of firm food (e.g., fish crackers).

F. Teach Correct Chewing: Teach the client to use the lateral margins of the tongue to hold food at the molars while chewing.

4. Stimulating High Lateral Elevation and Deep Midline Grooving

The tongue can be stimulated to elevate its sides very high while depressing the midline deeply by stimulating for the Tongue Gag Response (TGR).

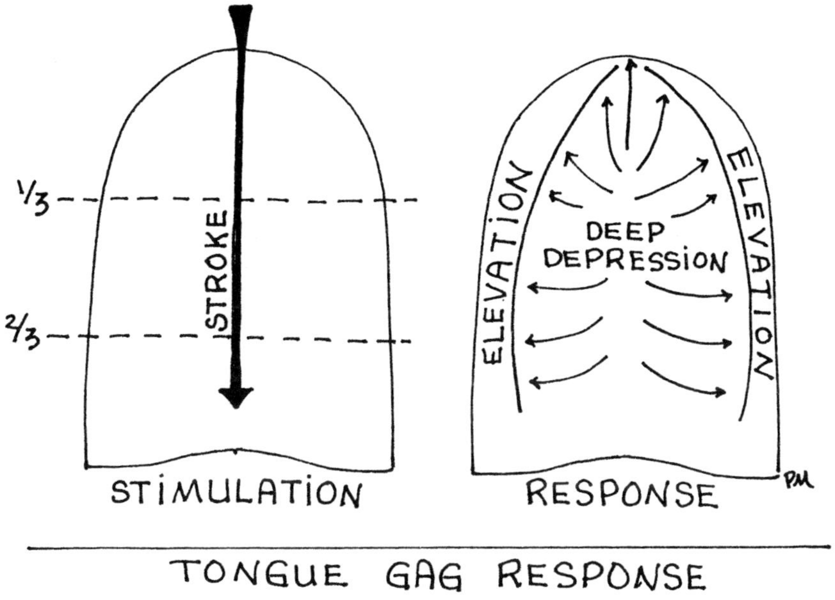

• Stimulation: Stimulate the tongue down the midline from the tip to the back 1/3. Use a textured object such as: finger, toothbrush, pretzel or other food, mouthing toy, Toothette, Nuk massage brush, Infa-Dent toothbrush.

• Response: The tongue: (1) elevates the sides, (2) depresses the middle, (3) stretches forward in the anterior 2/3, and (4) stretches backward in the posterior.

Gagging a client can be a very useful means of teaching him to take voluntary control of this movement pattern right away. Make sure that you use the gag only occasionally, and that you reassure him afterwards.

5. Stimulating Tip Elevation

The tip itself can be stimulated to elevate independently from the rest of the tongue:

A. Press Into the Tip: Place a firm object on the most anterior part of the tip of the tongue. Push into the tongue gently toward the back of the tongue so as to push the tip into the body of the tongue. Instruct the child to "push." Make sure to push until you feel the tongue resist your movement.

B. Brush the Tip: Use a rough object such as a toothbrush to brush in short strokes from the exact tip of the tongue towards the blade without stimulating the blade. Also brush from the exact tip towards the lateral margins of the tip without touching the blade.

C. Ask the Client to Push: Place an object (finger, tongue depressor, etc.) flat against the tip of the tongue and ask the client to push it out or away. Do not push the tip yourself. Use the gentle touch of your finger on the tip to give the client tactile stimulation to use as a goal for his own extension of the tip. By touching the tip only lightly, you will encourage the client to actively move the tip forward.

D. Press Downward: Place a firm object on top of the tongue-tip and press gently downward. Ask the client to push up.

E. Press into the Lateral Tip: Place a firm object on the lateral portion of the tongue-tip and ask the client to push it away toward the side. Make sure not to touch the blade's lateral margins. Repeat on both sides.

F. Lick Upward: Ask the client to lick up an object such as a lollipop or Popsicle. Make sure the client is licking upward with the tip and not the blade.

G. Protrude the Tongue: Ask the client to protrude the tongue tip.

6. Stimulating Back Lateral Margin Elevation

The back-lateral margins of the tongue will have to be stimulated to facilitate back-lateral stability as well as to produce /r/:

A. General Awareness: Use visual and tactile stimulation to teach the three sections of the tongue back — two lateral backs and a middle back.

B. Stimulate the Back Lateral Margins: Use a textured surface to stroke the lateral back margins of the tongue in short strokes. Use: a toothbrush, Toothette, Ora-Swab, Infa-Dent.

C. Bite Down and Push Up: Teach the client to bite down gently on the back lateral margins and to push upwards against the upper molars in the back with those parts. When the sides of the tongue elevate, the midline should depress forming the tongue into a bow-shaped position sometimes called the "butterfly" position. The mouth should open wide as the client pushes up higher and higher.

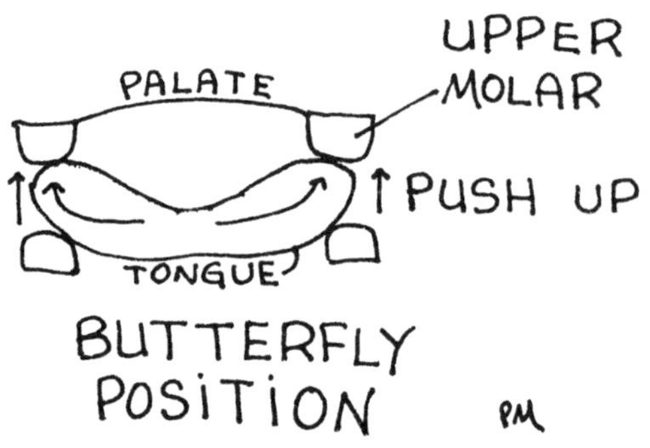

D. Practice Speech From This Position: Have the client practice a wide variety of speech events while holding the tongue in this position. Have him: read, recite, say single words, etc. The idea is to retrain the tongue to move from these points of stability.

7. Stimulating for Increased Tone In the Tongue

The overall muscle tone of the tongue can be increased when it is lax.

A. Increase Overall Whole Body Tone: When tone in the whole body is increased, tone in the tongue is as well.

B. Press Into the Tongue: Place a firm object (e.g., finger tip, toothette, tongue depressor) directly on the tip of the tongue and push inward gently but firmly. Ask the client to "push" against the object with the tongue. Make sure to place the object on the exact tip of the tongue, not on the top or the underside. In order for the client to attain enough pressure to push the object out of the mouth, he must tense up the entire tongue from back to tip. Use as much pressure (it will take very little) as needed to get the client to work the tongue into a tense single mass.

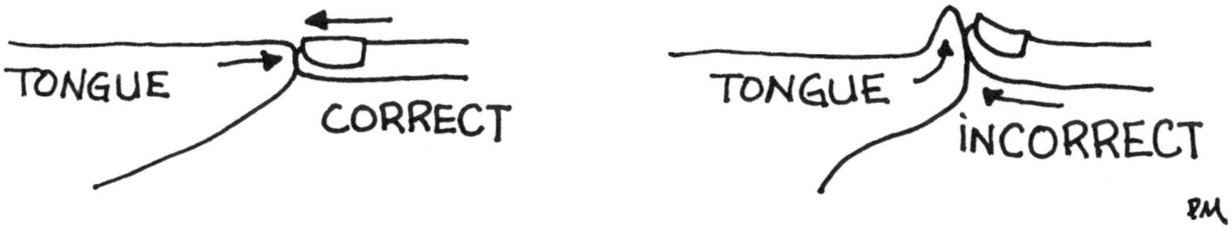

C. Squeeze the Tongue: This is a voluntary movement on the part of the client. Ask the client to stick out the tongue and to "squeeze it," or make it "narrow," "hard," "strong" or "tight."

D. Combine Squeeze and Push: Combine techniques B and C above to teach the client to push and squeeze together.

E. Squeeze and Push to the Alveolar Ridge: Challenge the client to push a raisin or sunflower seed up against the alveolar ridge by squeezing and pushing. Hold this position for increasing lengths of time to build the internal image of the position. Make sure he's using the tip and not the blade of the tongue.

F. Do Dental Floss Holder Curls: Use a dental floss holder as an object to pull against with the tongue tip. Curl the tip under and behind the floss. Pull the floss into the mouth in a curling fashion.

Chapter Six Summary

Chapter Six has presented techniques to facilitate improved tongue movements based on a new concept of tongue mobility. This new concept is based on palatography research and principles of movement development.

Chapter 7

Putting It All Together

Chapter Contents

1. Hierarchy of the Oral-Motor Approach
2. Developmental Apraxia
3. Severe Unintelligibility
4. The Frontal Lisp
5. The Lateral Lisp
6. Facilitating Back Phonemes /k/ and /g/
7. Facilitating Oral Movement for Phoneme /l/
8. Facilitating Oral Movement for Phoneme /r/

This chapter demonstrates how to incorporate oral-motor diagnostic and therapeutic concepts into selected aspects of articulation and phonological therapy. We begin with an organization of this material into a hierarchical approach, and then present several therapeutic programs for specific common articulation and phonological error patterns.

Hierarchy of the Oral-Motor Approach

A hierarchy for the oral-motor approach to articulation and phonological therapy has been conceived. This hierarchy is a hierarchy of thinking, meaning that it represents the sequence of thinking that a therapist should do both when planning a program of treatment and when designing individual therapy sessions.

This hierarchy is extremely flexible and should be incorporated appropriately to each individual client's needs and situation. It is not intended as a rigid formula to follow. Considering the given restrictions each client brings to therapy, therapists should adjust the course of treatment and the contents of individual treatment sessions to reflect the best possible situation for improving oral-motor and articulation skills.

The hierarchy has been divided into four sections: (1) address fundamental skills, (2) attend to the oral mechanism's environment, (3) facilitate improved oral habits, and (4) facilitate improved oral control for speech. To facilitate understanding, a final section on working through the hierarchy is included as a foundation for treatment.

1. Address Fundamental Skills

A. Provide Hip-Shoulder-Head-Neck Mobility and Stability: When the client has neuromuscular problems or gross and fine motor delay, consult with your team occupational and physical therapist regarding optimum movement activities and positioning that will be advantageous for improving movement postural stability and tone. Include this aspect of the program before or during articulation and phonological therapy.

B. Provide Normalization of Tactile Sensitivity: To facilitate more appropriate tactile responses to oral input in children with oral-tactile sensitivity problems, present systematic touch stimulation to the body, face and oral mechanism in order. Include this aspect of the program before or during articulation and phonological therapy.

C. Facilitate Respiratory/Phonatory Control: Make team decisions with OT/PT regarding optimum positioning and movement activities that will facilitate improved respiratory control. Include this aspect of the program before or during articulation and phonological therapy. Work to facilitate greater voluntary control of inhalation, exhalation, voicing, prolongation of sound, pitch and loudness variations, intonation patterns and rhythmic vowel productions. Use: inspiration-expiration spirometers, horns, whistles, sirens, kazoos, tubes, etc.

D. Facilitate Palatal Control: Work toward greater palatal control if that is a concern. Referral for a complete velopharyngeal evaluation may be necessary before or during articulation and phonological therapy. Utilize techniques from dysphagia literature and traditional cleft palate literature to facilitate velar elevation and control. Encourage development of bilabial, lingua-labial and velar fricatives (vocal pre-cursors of the fricatives.) Use: tubes, nasal clamps, lip retractors, etc., to help clients understand oral versus nasal airflow.

2. Attend to the Oral Mechanism's Environment

A. Eliminate Oral Habits: Eliminate thumbsucking, nail biting, pacifier sucking, clothes chewing, cheek sucking, lip licking, etc., before or during articulation and phonological therapy. Inappropriate oral movements and excessive pressures may interfere with oral-motor learning. "Set the stage" for the best possible oral control.

B. Refer to Medical, Surgical or Orthodontic Professionals: Eliminate or reduce the effects of deviant fistulas, frenums, clefts, structural insufficiencies, oral cancers, dental occlusion problems, upper respiratory problems, etc., before or during the course of treatment. "Set the stage" for the best possible oral control.

3. Facilitate Improved Oral Habits

A. Establish a "Normal" Oral Rest Position: Establish appropriate jaw, lip and tongue position for oral rest and the neutral position before or during articulation and phonological therapy.

B. Establish a "Normal" Swallow: Eliminate reverse swallow pattern; establish tongue bowling, lateralizing, retracting, forming a bolus, suctioning, "normal" swallow, and complete evacuation before or during articulation and phonological therapy.

4. Facilitate Improved Oral Control for Speech

A. Facilitate Jaw Mobility and Stability: Provide activities and techniques to increase and improve jaw mobility and stability before or during articulation and phonological therapy.

B. Facilitate Improved Face and Lip Control: Reduce lip retraction and provide techniques to stimulate, strengthen and improve voluntary control of lip movements before or during articulation and phonological therapy.

C. Facilitate Improved Tongue Control: Stimulate for improvements in tongue bowling, lateralization, back elevation, tip elevation and midline depression before or during articulation and phonological therapy.

D. Facilitate Phoneme Development: While oral-motor skills are improving, therapy is directed, of course, to facilitating sound emergence. Traditional articulation or phonological therapy practices and principles are included.

5. Work Through the Hierarchy

Understand the following when using the hierarchy as a foundation of treatment:

A. Some therapy can proceed before problems high on the hierarchy have been eliminated. For example, a client may need to be evaluated for a possible velopharyngeal closure problem, but such an exam cannot take place until a general physical exam takes place, a referral is made, and until insurance issues are handled. In such a case, oral-motor and articulation therapy can proceed even though it may be months until evaluation and medical treatment of the velar problem will take place. Other aspects of treatment can be addressed in the meantime.

B. Some therapy cannot proceed before problems high on the hierarchy have been eliminated. For example, little progress will be made with a frontal lisp if a child continues to have a strong thumbsucking habit, a strong reverse swallow pattern, an inappropriate oral rest position and a large anterior open bite. The therapist who attempts articulation therapy for the lisp under these conditions will be met with limited success in most cases. In some cases, articulation therapy should wait until these other factors are eliminated. In other cases, articulation therapy can proceed at the same time that these other factors are addressed.

Developmental Apraxia

The topic of developmental apraxia is far too complex to handle completely in a small section of information such as this. Therefore, we shall present an extremely simplified description of the disorder from a motoric perspective, and a simplified overview of the oral-motor therapy components of treatment.

Developmental apraxia is viewed in the motor literature as a sensorimotor integrative disorder which consists of problems in organizing incoming sensation from the tactile, vestibular and proprioceptive systems. The client with developmental apraxia of speech cannot organize that which he perceives through these sensory channels. Therefore, he cannot figure out how to make appropriate movements when they are needed. He has a so-called "motor planning problem" which can affect all movements.

The term "oral apraxia" suggests that the individual has difficulty planning out any oral movements, including those for speech, feeding, and imitation. The term "verbal apraxia" suggests that the individual has problems only in planning out the movements for speech.

The most important notion to center on in all of our discussions about developmental apraxia is that at its core, the problem is one of organizing sensation. This does not mean that the client has difficulty perceiving sensation, it means that once sensation is perceived, it is not well integrated with other incoming sensation and it is not properly stored. Thus, clients with developmental apraxia of speech have difficulty understanding how tactile, vestibular and proprioceptive sensations for producing speech are interrelated; their memory of oral position and movement is poor.

Children with developmental apraxia of speech often demonstrate at least the following patterns: (1) oral-tactile sensitivity disturbances, (2) muscle tone disturbances, (3) abnormal vestibular responses, (4) poor awareness of the oral mechanism, (5) poor differentiation of oral movements, (6) delayed oral-motor development, (7) deviant oral-motor patterns, (8) very poor control of oral movements, and (9) difficulty transferring oral movement into phoneme production.

Oral-motor therapy is an important part of treatment for the client with developmental apraxia of speech. Goals will include: (1) to normalize oral-tactile sensitivity, (2) to normalize muscle tone, (3) to normalize vestibular responses, (4) to increase awareness of the oral mechanism through multisensory learning activities, (5) to facilitate improved differentiation of oral movements, (6) to facilitate more advanced oral movements, (7) to inhibit abnormal oral movements, (8) to improve voluntary control of oral movements, and (9) to learn to transfer oral movement patterns into vocalizations and phoneme productions.

Severe Unintelligibility

A treatise on severe unintelligibility and phonological delay or disorder also is beyond the scope of a short section such as this. A few words on the topic are appropriate, however.

First, let us be clear in our understanding that a client with a "pure" phonological impairment should not show difficulties in oral-motor control. He should not demonstrate problems in: (1) muscle tone, (2) oral-tactile sensitivity, (3) oral awareness and control, (4) differentiation of oral movements, (5) vestibular responses, (6) delayed or deviant oral movement patterns, or (9) difficulty in transferring oral movement into phoneme production.

A "pure" phonological impairment is a language problem. After all, phonology is one aspect of language along with syntax and semantics. A client with a phonological delay or disorder has his problem because he does not understand or carry out the rules which govern the use of phonemes in language.

In my nearly 25 years of providing speech and language services to infants, toddlers, preschool and elementary age children, I have seen only a very few who fit this description. Almost all of the thousands of children I have seen who could be classified as having a phonological impairment have had difficulties with oral-tactile sensitivity, oral tone, oral awareness, differential control of oral movements, problems in oral stability and mobility, and the like.

Treatment for the client with severe phonological delay or disorder, therefore, takes on all the appearance of that for developmental apraxia of speech. The difference between severe phonological delay and developmental apraxia seems, for all practical purposes, to be merely one of degree.

All the techniques described in this book, therefore, are relevant to the client with severe phonological delay or disorder. Techniques to normalize oral-tactile sensitivity and to facilitate improved jaw, lip and tongue control help to bring fuller awareness, differentiation, maturity and control of oral movements for clients with phonological delay or disorder just as they do for other clients.

The Frontal Lisp

Although the frontal lisp has been considered a "mild" articulation error, it seems to be one that plagues many therapists and a problem which can be lifelong. The following overview of the disorder demonstrates how the hierarchy of thinking can be incorporated into the diagnosis and treatment of the frontal lisp.

1. When to Enroll the Client With a Frontal Lisp

Most therapists nationwide are waiting to enroll children with frontal lisps until they are much older — say in third or fourth grade. Too many children spontaneously grow out of the problem for therapists to devote much time and attention to them when children are young. Whether or not you take on a younger child with a frontal lisp probably has more to do with the size of your caseload, the policy (if you have one) of the therapists in your district or hospital division, and/or parental or teacher pressure.

• Implications for Therapy: Articulation and oral-motor therapy for the client with a frontal lisp can be addressed early. However, treatment logistics will prevent this in most cases.

2. The Tongue Probably Is Not "Too Big"

Many therapists describe children who demonstrate frontal lisps as having tongues that are "too big for their mouths." What appears to be a tongue that is "too big" is usually a tongue that is too flaccid. A tongue that is low in tone looks big and floppy and tends to be used very sloppily outside of the mouth. Low oral tone may be related to overall whole body hypotonicity.

Slightly low muscle tone which is present only in the oral mechanism will not interfere with any other motor control than that required for speech. Remember that speech consists of some of the finest motor movements that we humans do. Thus, when lower tone is only slight, it may show up only in the movements made by the mouth.

• Implications for Therapy: If low oral tone is at the base of the problem, then techniques to facilitate improved tone, especially in the tongue, are in order. All the stimulation techniques for the tongue which have been described in Chapter Six on the tongue will facilitate improved overall tone in the tongue.

3. Jaw Problems Are Likely

When the tongue protrudes during speech and/or feeding tasks, the problem often lies in the jaw. As we have described in the text, jaw control for speech needs to be finely "graded." The child has to have the ability to be able to control fine grades of opening and closing. He has to be able to open it only so far during production of certain sounds. The sibilants are a classic example of this: the jaw has to be held open just a little bit, not fully open and not fully closed.

• Implications for Therapy: Activities to facilitate improved jaw stability are appropriate.

4. Tongue Stability is a Problem

Stability of the tongue is a concern whether the problem lies in poor jaw control, or in low muscle tone of the tongue, or both. The tongue is not maintaining its neutral position inside of the mouth if it is being allowed to slip forward, and therefore tongue stability is lacking.

• Implications for Therapy: Techniques to facilitate improved tongue stability are in order. Use the butterfly position for this.

5. Differential Tongue Movement Problems are Likely

Most frontal lisps are the result of poor differentiation of tongue movements.

• Implications for Therapy: Activities and techniques to facilitate improved tongue movement differentiation — bowling, lateral elevation, spreading, tip elevation, back elevation, midline depression — are in order.

6. Medical Status May Be a Factor

Another reason that a child may have a frontal lisp has to do with medical status, especially upper respiratory problems. Children bothered by allergies and chronic upper respiratory disorders tend to breathe through their mouths and position their tongues forward in order to have enough interoral space to breathe. This forward tongue position will habituate to oral rest, swallow and speech.

• Implications for Therapy: Therapists need to make themselves very aware of these children's medical status and plan therapy accordingly. In the ideal situation, all medical problems will be eliminated before or during the course of treatment. Compensatory techniques must be taught when medical problems cannot be eliminated.

7. General Knowledge May be a Factor

Some children simply have never been told or encouraged to breathe out of their noses instead of their mouths. Some have never been told to speak with their tongues inside of their mouths.

• Implications for Therapy: Information about nose versus mouth breathing should be presented to the client and parents, and the client should be instructed on appropriate oral movements for speech. Traditional articulation therapy techniques can be the basis of treatment.

8. Poor Sensory Awareness is Common

Children with frontal lisps often have slightly depressed levels of oral tactile sensitivity (hyposensitivity).

• Implications for Therapy: Activities to normalize oral-tactile sensitivity are in order.

The Lateral Lisp

Although the lateral lisp has also been considered a "mild" articulation error, it seems to be one that plagues many speech and language pathologists and it too can be a lifelong problem for some clients. The following overview of the disorder demonstrates how the hierarchy of thinking goes into diagnosis and treatment of the lateral lisp.

1. The Basic Problem

The fundamental problem with the lateral lisp is one of inappropriate tongue position. In the following three situations, airflow is projected through the mouth in a diffuse and broad way causing the characteristic "lateral" sound quality. The addition of saliva in the mouth causes a characteristic "slushy" sound quality.

A. In most cases, the tongue is humped high somewhere along the midline from tip to back while the sides of the tongue are lax and low. The middle section braces upward against the palate and air escapes laterally.

B. In some cases, the entire front of the tongue — including tip and blade — are pressing upward against the palate preventing a midline groove. Air escapes laterally.

C. In less common cases, the entire tongue maintains a low position and braces itself along the lower lateral teeth; no articulation with the palate is made. In this case, air escapes broadly over the entire surface of the tongue giving a "lateral" sound.

2. The Causes

A. Tactile Hypersensitivity: In the case of tactile hypersensitivity, the client holds the tongue in the high-guard position of the tongue retraction response: the tongue is held high and back in order to protect the oropharyngeal area and to prevent a gag. Children who are not currently hypersensitive but were earlier in development may have learned to hold the tongue habitually in this position. Long-term ventilator use also can cause this position.

B. Instability: Children who are unstable in an upright position, either in sitting or standing, or who were unstable when they were learning speech, sometimes learn to hold the middle of the tongue upward against the palate to stabilize the head and to generate more tone in the upper body.

C. Upper Respiratory Control: Children with a significant history of chronic blockage of the nasal passageways (due to allergies, frequent colds, etc.) sometimes brace the mouth open for breathing by pushing the middle portions of the tongue upward against the palate. Then they breathe around the lateral margins and learn this position as their "neutral" position.

D. Jaw Instability: When the jaw is unstable, children sometimes learn to stabilize it with the middle of the tongue jammed up against the palate. As a result, the resting posture of the tongue is with a high midline and the back posture from which speech emerges is also with a high midline.

E. Orthodontia Problems: Many times jaw instability is the result of poor positioning between the upper and lower molars, and the resultant problems the client has in settling on one comfortable jaw position for biting and chewing. When the jaw is unstable, children sometimes learn to stabilize it with the middle of the tongue pushed up against the palate. Orthodontic management will be necessary.

F. Sucking Habits: Children with long term persistent oral sucking habits (thumb and finger sucking, pacifier use, etc.) continue to practice the infantile suckle-swallow pattern for longer than is "normal." This pattern exercises the strong upward movement of the middle of the tongue from the blade to the back.

3. The Treatment Hierarchy

A. Fix the "Fixables": In the ideal situation, all medical, dental and oral structural problems, as well as all oral habits, will be eliminated before the articulation work begins. That way articulation training begins afresh with a perfectly structured oral mechanism which is free of any interfering oral habits. In practicality, we must fix what we can fix, wait for what will be fixed later, and settle for what will never be fixed in our time together with the client.

Often we must settle for the less-than-perfectly-structured oral mechanism. In these cases we teach compensation, and, therefore, a decision must be made as to the client's ability to handle this level of therapy. We ask ourselves, "Is it worth the client's time?" and "Is it worth my time?" Maturity level, cognitive skills, motor control and motivational issues must be taken into consideration.

B. Begin with the Traditional Techniques: Most therapists start with a series of tried and true traditional techniques. Traditional techniques for the lateral lisp generally focus on teaching the client to reposition the tongue. This is a good place to begin. If the client can learn correct sibilant production when we teach tongue placement and auditory discrimination alone, then that is our most effective beginning point in therapy.

C. Incorporate Lessons from Developmental Articulation Research: There are lessons that can be learned from the study of articulation development in infants and toddlers which can positively affect our therapy for the lateralized sibilant. For example, one of the most useful techniques for the lateral lisp is to teach the client to substitute /th/ for /s/. The reasons why this technique works are: (1) it is easy to get airflow directed medially this way, (2) it is a developmentally-appropriate substitution, and (3) it is an easier oral movement. In both theory and practice, teaching a client to substitute /th/ for /s/ can lead to correct tongue positioning for /s/ later.

D. Incorporate Lessons from Developmental Phonological Research: Phonological research reveals that children follow a sequence of sibilant emergence as their oral-motor skills mature. The sequence infants and toddlers follow is reflected in the following:

1. Develop Postvocalic /t/: Begin with lessons on postvocalic /t/. Make sure the client is producing postvocalic /t/ correctly by place and manner. Use words with simple VC or CVC construction.

2. Place Strong Aspiration on the Final /t/: Teach the client to place strong aspiration on postvocalic /t/ in isolation and in words. Ask the client to make "lots of air."

3. Change Aspiration into Stridency: Adjust jaw position so that the excess air begins to sound more strident, changing the production to /ts/. Work on /ts/ in isolation.

4. Rehearse Words with Postvocalic /ts/: Practice word-final position /ts/ in morpheme groups. Use words with simple VCC and CVCC construction.

a. Plural: hats, lights, boats
b. Possessive: the cat's meow, Pat's car, it's the rat's
c. Third Person Regular Tense Verb Marker: eats, hits, bats
d. Contracted Copular to be: It's blue. That's a car.
e. Contracted Auxiliary to be: It's jumping. That's falling.

5. Facilitate Postvocalic /s/: Children often acquire postvocalic /s/ before they learn prevocalic /s/. The oral-motor control seems to be easier for postvocalic /s/. Rehearse words with simple VC and CVC construction with /s/ in the final position.

6. Rehearse /s/ in the Prevocalic Position: The client now should be ready to handle prevocalic /s/ in words.

7. Practice Word-Initial /s/-Blends: The client now is ready for the /s/-blends including /sp/, /st/, /sk/, /sm/, /sn/, /sl/, /sw/. Keep in mind that /st/ and /sn/ are probably going to be the hardest.

E. Use Oral-Motor Techniques When Needed: Correcting tongue positioning for sibilant production when there is a lateral distortion can be one of the most frustrating and difficult therapy problems for many clients. The lateral lisp is one that some clients "learn to live with" when articulation therapy has failed.

Oral-motor techniques for the lateral lisp address five basic areas: (1) normalizing oral-tactile sensitivity, (2) decreasing facial tone, (3) improving jaw mobility, (4) improving jaw-lip-tongue differentiation, and (5) stabilizing the tongue at the back-lateral margins.

When stabilizing the back lateral margins, work through a sequence toward production of midline sibilants:

1. Stimulate the Sides of the Tongue: Use a textured surface to stroke the lateral back margins of the tongue. Use a toothbrush, Toothette, Infa-Dent toothbrush, etc. Ask the client to do this to himself.

2. Bite Down on the Lateral Margins: Teach the client to bite down with the molars on the lateral margins of the tongue on both sides simultaneously.

3. Bite Down and Push Up: Teach the client to use the sides of the tongue to push upwards against the upper molars in the back. When the sides of the tongue elevate, the midline should depress forming the tongue into a bow-shaped position sometimes called the "butterfly" position. The mouth should open wide as the client pushes up higher and higher.

4. Adjust the Jaw: Ask the client to elevate the jaw so that there is less space between the tongue and the palate.

5. Try a Sibilant: When a client stabilizes the tongue at the lateral margins (achieves a butterfly position), he has established a gross form of the new tongue position. However, at first there is too much tension and too much activity on the part of the tongue.There must be action to strengthen the position; eventually, the new position will be a relaxed one. Use the new position to rehearse /s/. Tell the client not to worry about what the phoneme sounds like. Tell him it will be distorted and not really sound like /s/. Tell the client to rehearse it anyway. It is not the sound quality that is important right now, it is the tongue position.

6. Establish the New Position in Speech: Work at a connected speech level first. Practice rote speech events such as counting, saying the alphabet, saying an address, and so forth, to establish the tongue position as the key to the client's oral-motor pattern. Establish the concept that holding his tongue in this position is the most important area of his concern. Reward him well for holding it, no matter how sloppy his speech sounds. At this point, do not worry about what the sibilant sounds like. The way it sounds can be shaped later.

7. Return to Traditional Therapy: Now that the new tongue position is establishing, return to traditional techniques and lessons from infants and toddlers. Shape the acoustic quality of the sibilants, and train the client to control his output.

Facilitating Back Phonemes /k/ and /g/

The following describes how oral-motor therapy is incorporated into a program to facilitate development of back phonemes /k/ and /g/. The ideas are listed from least to most invasive.

1. Use a Prespeech Vocalization

Stimulate the velar fricative in vocal play since: (1) it is an oral-motor pattern which emerges early in infant development (at 4-to-6 months of age), (2) it is an easier movement to make with the back of the tongue against the velum, (3) it can be made loosely and "floppy" with sustained airflow which seems to be easier than the movements needed for the stops, (4) it can be shaped easily into /k/, and (5) voice can be added to shape it into /g/. In some cases, we allow a child to use the velar fricative as an acceptable variation of /k/ or /g/ for some time.

2. Alter the Child's Body Positioning

Have the client lie in supine so that gravity will pull the whole tongue back into the oropharyngeal area. This position is more conducive to tongue-velum contact. Add flexion to the child's position in supine to draw the tongue and jaw up and back into close approximation to the palate. This gives a mechanical advantage to the production of /k/ and /g/ or the velar fricative.

3. Use Tactile Stimulation

Use the Tongue Retraction Response to stimulate the tongue to move back and elevate high toward the velum. Stroke down the midline of the tongue toward the back. At the tongue's half-way point (half-way back), the tongue should begin to pull itself up and back toward the velum. Ask the client to exhale while the stimulus is maintained. This will result in production of a velar fricative. The upward and backward movement of the tongue can be brought under voluntary control. Use verbal descriptions, hand gestures, pictures, etc., to bring multisensory awareness of the movement. Shape the production into /k/ and /g/.

4. Use Proprioceptive Stimulation

Apply deep pressure to the posterior tongue at midline and ask the child to "push up" against your finger. This is a "drastic" measure that should be saved for times when nothing else works. Press gently but somewhat firmly: be careful! Pressure provides the proprioceptive stimulation needed to teach the child to push the back of the tongue up. This technique is especially effective with interoral tactile hyposensitivity.

5. Use a Dysphagia Technique

Take hold of the tongue tip and blade by holding it with gauze and pull it forward gently while asking the client to pull the tongue back and in. This is another "drastic measure" which should be reserved for use when nothing else has worked. Pull the tongue out to stimulate backward movement of the tongue. When the tongue retracts, ask the client to blow gently over the top. The velar fricative should result.

6. Employ Traditional Articulation Techniques

When employing oral-motor techniques, don't forget to include traditional auditory and visual teaching methods.

Facilitating Oral Movement for Phoneme /l/

The following presents methods for incorporating oral-motor techniques into therapy designed to facilitate the emergence of /l/.

1. Stabilize the Jaw: Most cases of delayed /l/ emergence are related to an unstable jaw. When the jaw is unstable, the client will attempt /l/ production with the jaw and not the tongue. Techniques to increase awareness and control of the jaw are in order, as are those to facilitate jaw stability, in order to facilitate separate jaw and tongue movements.

2. Facilitate Tongue Differentiation: All the techniques for the tongue will help differentiate the tongue and its movements from that of the jaw.

3. Strengthen Tip Elevation: Sometimes clients use the blade instead of the tip of the tongue for elevation to the alveolus for /l/. Employ techniques to help differentiate and strengthen the tip from the body of the tongue.

4. Tone the Tongue: Sometimes clients "flop" the tongue for production of /l/. Utilize resistance techniques to the tongue to take the "flop" out of /l/ and to facilitate better overall tone in the tongue.

5. Do "Tongue Curls": Use a dental floss holder and have the client do curls with them by sticking the tongue tip behind the dental floss and curling the tip upward and back into the oral cavity. These, too, will tone the tongue.

6. Employ Traditional Articulation Techniques: When employing oral-motor techniques, don't forget to include traditional auditory and visual teaching methods.

Facilitating Oral Movement for Phoneme /r/

Long term persistent problems with production of consonantal and vocalic /r/ almost always are an oral-motor problem. These clients simply cannot figure out how to position the tongue for /r/, cannot achieve enough tenseness in the tongue for /r/, and cannot do either consistently to produce an /r/ with a good "ring!" to it.

Phoneme /r/ can be taught either as a "high back" /r/ in which the back lateral margins of the tongue elevate high, or as a "retroflex /r/" in which the tip of the tongue curls back toward the velum. Either form is an acceptable allophonic variation of /r/.

Clients who have been in long term /r/ therapy, typically are being taught to produce a high-back /r/, and this method is proving unsuccessful for them. The problem they encounter is that they are lifting the middle back and not the lateral backs of the tongue for the sound. When told to "lift the back," they are, but it's the wrong part. The distorted /r/ sound they produce is not an acceptable variation, and it is not a close approximation which can be shaped. It is the wrong sound!

The following demonstrates how oral-motor therapy can be incorporated into the diagnosis and treatment of the persistent long term /r/ distortion.

1. Oral-Motor Characteristics of the Distorted /r/

A. Slightly Low Tone in the Tongue: The tongue frequently looks soft, mushy, shaky and fasciculating.

B. Slightly Low Facial/Lip Tone: The face and lips frequently look soft, "marshmallow-like"; low tone is slight to excessive.

C. Jaw Instability: The jaw is allowed to drop too low or moves too much.

D. Slight Oral-Tactile Hyposensitivity: If oral-tactile sensitivity is a problem, it tends to be of a hyposensitive nature.

2. The Basic Problem of the Distorted /r/

The following list summarizes typical problems with /r/:

A. The tongue stays flat and immobile.
B. The tongue does not tense.
C. The tongue back does not elevate.
D. The client uses anterior instead of posterior tongue movement.
E. The client pushes the tongue tip into bottom teeth and braces there.
F. The client tenses the throat, shoulders, eyes, face or hands and not the tongue.
G. The client elevates the middle back instead of the lateral backs.

H. The client pulls the soft palate down instead of the tongue up and sounds hypernasal.

I. The client uses a forward overall tongue position.

M. The client uses high elevation of the middle, touches the palate and produces /g/.

N. The back of tongue goes down, or

O. The client uses the lips instead of tongue substituting /w/ for /r/.

3. Treatment Sequence

Therapy to help a client with a long-term, persistent "R" can be assisted when oral-motor techniques are included.

A. Fix the "Fixables": Attend to and eliminate structural and medical differences which may be contributing to the /r/ distortion. The most common problems seen are high arched palate and tight lingua frenum.

B. Begin with Traditional Techniques: Most therapy for "R", even if there are suspected oral-motor problems, usually begins with a series of traditional articulation therapy techniques that have proven useful for clients through the years. These are done first to screen out those clients who do not need an oral-motor component to their treatment. Traditional articulation therapy assumes that the client will be able to perform the actions described below with only the aid of verbal descriptions and visual models.

1. The Retroflex "R": The Retroflex "R" is made by curling the tip of the tongue up and back behind the alveolar ridge toward the juncture of the hard and soft palates but not touching the palates.

2. The "L-to-R Slide": Ask the client to produce an /l/, then to maintain voicing and contact with the palate while sliding the tongue-tip back toward the soft palate. This essentially positions the tongue in the Retroflex "R" position.

3. The "Z-to-R Slide": Have the client make a /z/, and then maintain voicing while sliding the tip of the tongue back toward the soft palate. This technique also trains the retroflex tongue position.

4. /w/-/l/-/r/ Sequence: Ask the client to say "wuh" and feel the lip movement. Ask the client to say "luh" and feel the tongue movement. Then ask the client to do the same tongue movement but reach back toward the soft palate instead of reaching for the alveolar ridge. An allophonic variation of /r/ should result.

5. Coarticulatory Effects: Use /gr/, /kr/, /ir/, and /yr/: Facilitate /r/ production by rehearsing it in pairs with other back sounds so that the tongue, already high in the back for production of these sounds, will more readily elevate up and back for /r/.

6. Focus on the Syllable: Once an excellent "R" is achieved through traditional means, work intensely at the syllable level. Use the vowel quadrilateral as your basis for choosing CV and VC combinations with "R". Select syllables in which you hear consistent success on "R" and rehearse these in drill. Use this time for intensive ear training, and make sure your client knows "This is perfect." DO NOT REWARD APPROXIMATIONS IF YOUR CLIENT HAS BEEN IN LONG-TERM THERAPY.

7. Focus on Speed: Substantial time spent on diligent practice of nonsense syllables helps the client make the transformation from single phonemes to words because the phonetic context is highly controlled. The key is to help the client say the syllables they can say in sequences with ever greater speed. By adding speed or rate without sacrificing quality of production, you will help the client transit from all vowels and consonants into and out of /r/ with greater efficiency and control.

8. Watch Retroflex /r/ Change into High Back /r/: Over time and as he gains strength and control over the lateral lift needed for the correct acoustic quality of /r/, the client will gradually shift from a retroflex /r/ into a neutral position /r/.

C. Use Oral-Motor Therapy Techniques if Needed to Normalize and Mature the Oral-Motor System: When traditional methods prove impossible, or when a client can achieve an acceptable /R/ occasionally but never consistently, it is time to look closely at his oral-motor abilities. Oral-motor techniques for the long-term /r/ client contain five basic components: (1) normalizing oral-tactile sensitivity, (2) increasing facial and oral tone, (3) stabilizing the jaw, (4) improving tongue-jaw differentiation, and (5) increasing tone or strength of the tongue. One or more of these areas will need to be addressed.

1. Normalize Oral-Tactile Sensitivity and Discrimination: Use oral-exploratory play activities to help the client become sensitive to incoming tactile stimulation and to increase his ability to perceive the separate oral parts.

2. Increase Facial and Oral Tone: Use techniques to increase lip and facial muscle tone. These will have a positive effect on increasing tone in the tongue.

3. Stabilize the Jaw: Use self-monitoring, resistance and external stability to help the client become aware of his jaw movements and to stabilize the jaw in a partly open position.

4. Improve Tongue-Jaw Differentiation: Stabilize the jaw in a large open position and perform tongue movements and exercises. These will help the client learn to move the tongue without help from the jaw.

5. Increase Tongue Strength: Use a dental floss holder to do "Tongue Curls." These will help bring up the tip and will help increase tone in the tongue. They also will help to differentiate the tongue's movements from that of the jaw.

D. Teaching Retroflex /r/: Sometimes we can skip those techniques and activities in section C above and move directly to using oral-motor techniques to achieve an /r/.

1. Do Curls: Place the string of a dental floss holder across the tongue blade. Ask the client to curl up the tongue tip while you gently tug outward on the holder. This step gives the client a slight bit of resistance to upward curling of the tongue which makes the tongue's movements in this direction become more salient to him: he can perceive the movement better because he is getting more proprioceptive input from the movement. The tug of resistance also makes the upward movement of the tip more organized.

2. Reach and Push: Place the dental floss holder's curved surface up against the hard palate at about the juncture of the hard and soft palate. Ask the client to curl up the tongue tip and touch the string, and gently push back against the string. This should tense up the tongue and place it in a fairly good position. Then ask the client to vocalize. If all goes well, you should hear a fairly close /r/.

3. Reach, Push and Vocalize: Repeat Step 2 with one change — ask the client to vocalize as he elevates the tongue tip to the string. The client should say "ar". Now you have a VC combination with which to work, and you can return to traditional articulation techniques.

E. Teaching High Back /r/: Teaching the high-back /r/ is considerably more difficult for most clients. The client must learn to elevate the lateral back margins of the tongue very high while keeping the midline depressed, and while tensing the entire tongue.

1. Push: Place the dental floss holder (without the string) on the back of the tongue so that its two blunt prongs are touching the back lateral margins of the tongue.

2. Push Upward: Ask the client to push upward against the blunt prongs with the parts of the tongue which are touching the prongs.

3. Bite and Push: Teach the client to bite down on the back lateral margins and to push up against the molars as he did against the dental floss holder in #2 above. Push high to create high lateral walls and a low midline.

4. Bite-Push-Vocalize: Repeat #2 above and vocalize. The resultant sound should not be /r/ — it should be a distorted vowel-like sound.

5. Bite-Push-Vocalize-Adjust Backward: Repeat #4 above and then slide the lateral back sides of the tongue backward along the molars to tuck them in behind the molars. Check the vocal quality which results to determine if the client is achieving the sound quality of a good /r/ sound. Continue to adjust until an acoustically-correct /r/ is heard.

6. Adjust Jaw Position: Slowly and gently adjust the elevated or depressed position of the jaw in order to make adjustments in the acoustic quality. In many cases, the jaw is unstable and needs to me stabilized. Have the client bite down on a Toothette handle or craft stick to settle jaw position during this work.

7. Adjust Lip Position: Alter lip position forward and back to achieve correct tongue position and acoustic quality. Lip protrusion will pull the tongue slightly forward, and lip retraction will pull it back and create a tighter position.

8. Return to Traditional Techniques to Work on Movement Sequences: Once an acoustically acceptable /r/ is produced, return to traditional articulation therapy techniques to work on syllables. Teach the client to transition into and out of correct /r/ position with all vowels. Focus on "perfect" acoustic qualities for both /r/ and the vowels: don't let the client get slur or distort AT ALL from producing syllables too fast.

9. Increase Speed: Continue #8 above with gradually increasing speed. Again, do not sacrifice sound perfection as speed increases.

Chapter Seven Summary

In Chapter Seven we have presented ways in which oral-motor techniques can be incorporated into articulation and phonological therapy for a variety of common problematic cases.

Annotated Bibliography of Selective References

The following presents a list of selected bibliographical references readers can use to begin their own research into oral-motor therapy. This is not an all-inclusive reference list. Instead, it is a list of some of the best materials available in each area.

Apraxia

Marshalla, Pamela. Becoming Verbal with Developmental Apraxia. Marshalla Speech and Language, 11417 - 124th Ave NE, Kirkland, WA 98033. 425-828-4361. •A one-of-a-kind book written for professionals and parents who live and work with children withdevelopmental apraxia. Presents five stages of imitation development as they apply in the facilitation of speech and language skills in non-verbal and minimally-verbal apraxic children. (2001)

Feeding and Dysphagia Therapy

Logemann, Jerilyn. Evaluation and Treatment of Swallowing Disorders. College-Hill Press, San Diego, CA. •This now-classic text on assessment and programming for adult swallowing problems contains an excellent presentation of the stages of the mature adult swallow. Oral-motor exercises and stimulation techniques are scattered throughout. (1983)

Morris, Suzanne Evans and Marsha Dunn Klein. Pre-Feeding Skills. Therapy Skill Builders, A Division of Communication Skill Builders, 3830 E. Bellevue/P.O. Box 42050, Tucson, AZ 85733 (602) 323-7500. •Morris has several books on feeding therapy, but this collaboration with Dunn Klein certainly is her "must-have" text. Widely considered the "Bible" of feeding therapy, it covers: normal development, assessment, mealtime environments, positioning and handling, nutrition, therapy techniques, tube feeding, issues in cleft palate, and available pre-feeding materials. (1988)

"Skills Needed by Speech-Language Pathologists Providing Services to Dysphagic Patients/ Clients," in AHSA Vol. 32 (Suppl. 2), 7-12. •This typical all-inclusive position statement is must-reading for SLP's involved in dysphagia management. (1988)

Examination

Dworkin, James Paul and Richard Culatta. D-COME-T: Oral Mechanism Examination and Treatment. Available through Speech Dynamics, Inc., 41715 Enterprise Circle North, Suite 107, Temecula, CA 92590 (800) 337-9049. •This thorough examination and treatment protocol covers a complete program of assessment and treatment of oral-motor dysfunction.

Oral Cuing Systems

Vaughn, G. and Clark, R.M. Speech Facilitation. Charles C. Thomas, Springfield, IL. •If you want to find out what motokinesthetics is all about, this is the text that is currently available. It presents extraoral and intraoral tactile cues and guidelines for positioning the mouth for speech. The first chapter is a nice summary of what is known about the oral-tactile system. (1979)

Young, E. H. and Hawk, S. S. Motokinesthetic Speech Training. Stanford University Press, Stanford, CA. •This book presents the original oral-tactile cuing system. You may find a copy in the stacks of a nearby university library. (1955)

Oral-Motor Techniques in Articulation Therapy

Marshalla, Pamela. "The Role of Reflexes in Oral-Motor Learning: Techniques for Improved Articulation." In Seminars in Speech and Hearing, Vol. 6 No. 4 Nov 1985. •The author's first attempt to put down in print what she does in therapy that works. Discusses the role of the tongue bowl response, the tongue lateralization response, and the gag reflex in the development of tongue movements for specific articulation deficits. (1985)

Orofacial Myology

"The role of the speech-language pathologist in assessment and management of oral myofunctional disorders." In ASHA Supplement #5. •This position statement is must-reading for the SLP involved in orofacial myofunctional disorders. (1991)

Hanson, M. and Richard H. Barrett. Fundamentals of Orofacial Myology. Charles C. Thomas, Springfield, IL. • This book presents the most current information one can find in text form on basic orofacial myology. This is the place to go to determine whether or not you want to become a certified orofacial myologist. It brings to you the scope of the practice and the fundamentals of treatment. (1989)

Phonology

Hodson, B.W. and Paden, E. P. Targeting Intelligible Speech. College-Hill Press, San Diego, CA. •If you are looking for an easy-to-read introduction to phonologically-based articulation therapy, this is the book. It combines a rather "cookbook" approach with sound theoretical foundations. You will learn how to do good phonologically-based articulation therapy from this little book. (1983)

Saliva/Drooling Management

Johnson, Hilary and Amanda Scott. A Practical Approach to Saliva Control. Communication Skill Builders. •This is the most comprehensive presentation available on how to manage a problem with saliva control. Presents assessment and treatment approaches, and discusses treatment from various perspectives: medial, surgical, and through speech, feeding, occupational and physical therapy. (1993)

Marshalla, Pamela. How to Stop Drooling. Marshalla Speech and Language, 11417 - 124th Ave., Kirkland, WA 98033 •This practical book presents techniques for handling problematic drooling. It includes activities and techniques for reducing drooling in the home, school or clinic. Directly applicable to therapy and highly useful for the speech-language, occupational and physical therapist. (1998)

Sanitary Procedures

"AIDS/HIV: Implications for the Speech-Language Pathologist and Audiologist." In ASHA Vol 31 June-July. •Must-reading for SLP's using oral stimulation. Summarizes precautions and legal issues regarding the SLP's role in preventing the spread of infectious disease. (1989)

Sensory, Motor and Sensorimotor Theory and Therapy

Ayres, A. Jean. Sensory Integration and the Child. Western Psychological Services, 12031 Wilshire Blvd, Los Angeles, CA 90025. •This is the best place to begin reading about sensorimotor integration and its relationship to oral movement. Written for parents, but most appropriate for the SLP. (1980)

Ayres, A. Jean. Sensory Integration and Learning Disorders. Western Psychological Services, 12031 Wilshire Blvd., Los Angeles, CA 90025. •After you've read Ayres (1980), dig into this for more concrete theoretical foundations about the sensory systems. Must-reading for therapists working with apraxia, learning disorders, and other forms of severe speech-language delay/disorder. (1978)

Ginsberg, Herbert and Sylvia Opper. Piaget's Theory of Intellectual Development. Prentice-Hall, Inc., Englewood Cliffs, NJ. •This is a great beginner reader on Piaget's work in intelligence which contains his theory that all early learning is a sensory and motor process.

Langley. M. Beth and Linda J. Lombardino (Eds.) Neurodevelopmental Strategies for Managing Communication Disorders in Children with Severe Motor Dysfunction. Pro-Ed, Austin, TX. •This text contains probably the best chapter on NDT that I have ever seen anywhere including what it is and how therapists go about implementing it. It also contains excellent chapters on other aspects of oral-motor and related functions: the respiratory system, prespeech assessment and treatment strategies, alternate feeding methods, nutrition, and sensory preparation of the oral mechanism. (1991)

Wilbarger, Patricia and Julia Leigh Wilbarger Sensory Defensiveness in Children Aged 2-12, An Intervention Guide. Avanti Educational Programs, 642 Island View Dr., Santa Barbara, CA 93109. •This book describes an aggressive brushing approach to reduce tactile sensitivity levels in children with severe tactile hypersensitivity and tactile defensive behavior.

Temporomandibular Joint

Kaplan, Andrew S. and Gray Williams, Jr. The TMJ Book. Pharos Books. 200 Park Avenue, New York, NY. •A great overview of the diagnostic and treatment components of temporomandibular joint problems. Written for the lay person but an excellent first source for the speech and language pathologist. (1988)

Thumbsucking

Marshalla, Pamela, How to Stop Thumbsucking. Marshalla Speech and Language, 11417 - 124th Ave. NE, Kirkland, WA 98033. •Written for both professionals and parents, this book presents information about why and how to go about eliminating thumbsucking and other oral habits. (2001)

Tongue

Lynch, Joan I. "Tongue Reduction Surgery: Efficacy and Relevance to the Profession." In ASHA Vol 32. •A basic introduction to tongue reduction surgery that does not include any descriptions of the actual procedures. Ends with an extensive bibliography for those seeking more information. (1990)

Boshart, Charlotte. A Treatise on the Tongue. Speech Dynamics, Inc., 41715 Enterprise Circle North, Suite 107, Temecula, CA 92590 (800) 337-9049. •This book presents a wide variety of information about the tongue including: movement, muscles, nerves, structure, tongue size and growth, tongue surface, tactile and taste sensitivity, stabilization, the lingua frenum, and more. (1999)

Fletcher, Samuel G. Articulation: A Physiological Approach. Singular Publishing Group, Inc. 4284 41st Street, San Diego, CA 92105-1197. •This book presents an excellent description of tongue movements for articulation.

Vocal (Pre-speech) Development

Oller, David Kimbrough. Infant Vocalizations and the Development of Speech. In Allied Health and Behavioral Science Journal, 1 (14). •This article summarizes the basics of vocal development in infants as it has been parcelled out up until that point. It is an excellent place from which to begin the study of oral movement development as it is reflected in vocal development. (1978)

More Books by Pam Marshalla

How to Stop Thumbsucking **$14.95**
How to Stop Drooling **$14.95**

Pam Marshalla's How-to Series gives you easy-to-understand resources that help to reduce or eliminate your child's thumbsucking and excessive drooling. Includes practical guidelines, solutions, and activities for home or therapy.

Becoming Verbal with Childhood Apraxia **$19.95**
New Insights on Piaget for Today's Therapy

Particularly relevant for minimally verbal children who have been diagnosed with apraxia or dyspraxia of speech. Includes the organization and facilitation of early sound and word emergence.

Oral Motor Techniques in Articulation and Phonological Therapy **$49.95**

Includes all the basics of oral-motor therapy for improving jaw, lip, and tongue control, and for normalizing oral-tactile sensitivity. Written for both the professional and student speech-language pathologist, the text guides the reader through fundamental techniques used in treatment. An excellent supplimental text for courses on motor speech disorders, articulation, phonology, feeding, and dysphagia.

Successful R Therapy **$49.95**

Learn how to train the most difficult R clients. From the cornerstone R to conversational speech, this takes you through every stage of articulation therapy for the misarticulated R. Includes deep insights into the relationships between oral-motor skills, auditory processing and articulation control.

Order Today

1 Select titles

2 Find total

3 Mail order

Title	Price	Quantity	Total
How to Stop Thumbsucking	$14.95		$
How to Stop Drooling	$14.95		$
Becoming Verbal with Developmental Apraxia	$19.95		$
Oral-Motor Techniques	$49.95		$
Successful R Therapy	$49.95		$
Wholesale prices available on request			
U.S. shipping (1–4 books = $3.95; 5–10 books = $7.50)			$
International shipping (1–4 books = $9.95; 5–10 books = $14.95)			$
WA residents add 8.9% sales tax			$
Total			**$**

Send check or money order to
Marshalla Speech and Language
11417 - 124th Ave NE, #202
Kirkland, WA 98033

Questions?
(425) 828-4361

www.pammarshalla.com

Name:____________________

Street:____________________

City:____________________

State:________ Zip: ________

Phone: (____)____________

E-mail:____________________

MSL
Marshalla Speech and Language